STOP THIS GAME

STOP THIS GAME

My Life with Bipolar Disorder

Jaka Tomc

Copyright © 2023 Jaka Tomc

All rights reserved.

This book is not meant as a substitute for medical advice. If you encounter issues with your mental health, please seek professional help.

No part of this book may be reproduced, stored in a retrieval system, or transmitted in any form or by any means, electronic, mechanical, photocopying, recording, or otherwise, without the express written permission of the publisher.

Copy editor: Beth Bazar

To bipolars. Never surrender.

A Day I Will Never Forget

:):

"I'm swallowing the pills!" I yelled at my mother. I grabbed the box of lithium and poured its contents into a glass of water. The pills (I guess it was my lucky day) didn't dissolve, but I managed to swallow some.

"Are you happy now?" she asked.

I don't remember my answer, and it doesn't matter. A minute later I was locked in the bathroom, throwing all the clothes into the washing machine. Actually, it wasn't just clothes. Anything I could grab found its way into the opening. Everything needed to be washed and cleansed of negative energy. If I could have, I would've squeezed myself inside. Instead I took off my clothes and stepped into the bathtub. I filled it with hot water and lay down. The water relaxed me, but only for a few seconds. I felt the rage coming back. Somebody probably said something on the other side of the door. Looking at the situation now, my mother and uncle, who were in my apartment at the time, probably thought I was cutting my veins. I'd think of that if it was my kid in a similar situation.

"Jaka, come out," said my uncle.

"No! I'm not coming out or going anywhere!"

In the next moment, my fist was lodged in the door. I pulled it out. There was no going back now. My future was determined. An all-inclusive retreat was waiting for me. Again.

But to better understand the scene, we must step back. We won't go far. Let's move twenty-four hours back in time. Excuse me if I don't remember specific events or if I present them a little differently than they actually happened. My memory is full of holes, and a lot of stuff was knowingly or unknowingly stored in my subconscious. Maybe some of you are trying to figure out why I started with this episode, which wasn't the first one. The answer is simple. It was the worst. I did encounter stronger manias after that, but I was better prepared for them. They also left a less-severe aftermath. Let's go back to when everything was peachy, and I was full of positive expectations.

I was sitting at Maček (Cat) café. Maček (when it still existed) was my favorite place besides Daktari. It just felt like home. The energy was friendly, and I knew the staff and always met other people. I was sitting outside (I never had a favorite table, so I always sat randomly), drinking a nonalcoholic beverage. There is a slight chance I was drinking Jameson and Schweppes, a drink I named Sandokan a few years later. But I probably drank Cedevita or an orange squeezed into a half-liter glass of water.

It all depended on how much money I carried at a particular moment. The contents of my wallet usually disappeared at each place I visited.

While chilling at Maček, I checked Facebook to see how many people were RSVP'ing to my party. There was a lot of interest, and I planned to publish my second book, *Manic Poet*, on the same day. The plan was simple. A hundred copies were being printed, and I would sell them or give them away at the party. There was another plan. A more daring one that included a white van and members of an airsoft unit that were supposed to bring me to the party or kidnap me there. I dropped that plan before I could seriously contemplate it.

Suddenly, my mobile phone rang. The printer was talking about my books. Something wasn't right. I don't remember the conversation, but I remember walking up and down the street, yelling into the phone like a wounded animal. People were clearing the path for me, jumping away. I was acting like I was all alone in the world. Actually, I was. It was one of the loneliest days ever.

My family appeared out of nowhere. I wasn't alone anymore. Unfortunately, my mania was so intense by then that I couldn't sit in one place. I cruised the tables, talked to strangers, and walked the nearby alleys.
My folks were waiting for me in vain.

Then the books appeared. The first hundred copies of my biography, my failed attempt to describe life with bipolar disorder. The party had begun. Not the real one. That one was in the future and at a different venue.

I'm talking about the party in my mind. A party that transforms you into a ticking bomb.

The books were amateur. They were made with a desktop printer and held together with staples. Maybe that was the deal. The guy probably did his best in the short time I had given him. It didn't matter. I had the first copies and started giving them to random people. To whoever was interested. I also signed them. When everyone had a copy, I stuffed the rest into the stand with free magazines. Who wouldn't want to take a piece of me? Who wouldn't want to know what was inside my crazy mind? Who wouldn't like to hear my story?

It was late—time to go home. I took about thirty copies of my precious book and handed them to strangers on the streets of Ljubljana. I threw some of them on the ground in Prešeren Square and a few into the Ljubljanica River. Why? Because it seemed like a great idea at the time. Even the fish should read it! If I remember correctly, I spent the night at my parents' place. That means I boarded the bus for Ljubljana the following day, got off the bus in Trzin (about ten kilometers away from my home), and walked the rest of the way.

It was anything but boring. I thought I could create wind with my hands, move clouds, and even teleport. I made a few short stops, talked to strangers, jumped the fence of a random house, and found a bag with a fresh sandwich inside. Of course, I ate it, happy that the universe was taking good care of me. I stopped at the bar, where I demonstrated my teleportation abilities to a group of youngsters, and headed home. I wrote a short post for Facebook about two coworkers living at my place until they found a new apartment. I'd kicked them out two days earlier, thinking they were drug dealers.

Has anybody seen X and Y? I want them to return my keys, mobile phone, and passport. The chick is redheaded with glasses, and the fellow is handsome and unshaven.

So, we're back at the beginning of this story. My mother, my uncle, and I were in the apartment. We all knew how this would play out at that moment—or no one did. I was trying desperately to break the cycle I was in then—a cycle that looked like this: mania, intervention, hospitalization, depression, remission, mania. I had to do something. That's why I swallowed the pills. That's why I broke the door. That's why I stormed out, threw my keys in the middle of the road, climbed the floodgate,
and gazed into the roaring river. I cried my heart out.
When we were children, we said, "Stop this game!" if we didn't want to play anymore. I wanted the game to stop. I wanted out.

Luckily I didn't go out that day. I went in. My fourth visit to the psychiatric hospital went smoothly. I'm talking about admission—a check by a psychiatrist-on-call who determines whether you can return home or need to be admitted. In my case, the decision was a piece of cake. I tried to act normal, but the mania was too intense. I probably did something while undressing or later in the smoking room. That memory is perhaps gone for good. I remember waking up daily, wondering why I was still strapped to the hospital bed. You've read it correctly. I'm talking about days, not hours. Every four hours (day and night), they must check you out and decide whether you're ready to be unstrapped. I just wasn't. Not the second day, not the fourth one, not the seventh one, and not the tenth. I was immobilized for eleven days. Eleven! That's longer than Slovenia's war for independence. You might be wondering how I went to the toilet. I didn't. They unstrap one of your hands so you can eat, and that's about it. Don't get me wrong; I'm not blaming anyone. It's just the hospital's protocol. I was probably dangerous at that time to myself and others. In some other countries, they would have thrown me into a padded room. In Slovenia, straps were popular at that time.

Are you still wondering why I started this book on that particular day? Because I'll remember it forever. It was Friday, August 13, 2010, and I was celebrating the thirtieth anniversary of my birth, tied to a bed and absolutely alone.

August/September 2010

:):

August 13, 2010

The patient is admitted to our hospital for the fourth time. He came here from his home without a referral. The doctor-on-call stated on admittance:

The patient says that he's not agitated, that he's not sick, and that everything is screwed. He's celebrating his 30th birthday today. It's awful. He doesn't know how to move on. He says cameras are everywhere, and they can see him and everyone else. He's Dr. Roth's patient. She's the reason for everything happening to him. He's taking Quilonorm. He took Depakine. He takes his medicine according to instructions.

Hetero-anamnesis:
The mother says he's been feeling worse since Sunday. For the last two days, he's been agitated, walking around, angry, and sleeping for about an hour and a half.

Status:
The patient is lucid, oriented, pressured speech,

incoherent, paranoid, delusional, alluded, accusatory, elevated mood, very tense, agitated, and restless, but he accepts his hospitalization. Hard to talk to.

On admittance, the patient is not auto-aggressive, but hetero-aggression is possible due to high agitation.

Medical opinion:
The patient is admitted to a secured department for reintroduction of treatment in a manic state with psychotic symptoms. The patient has bipolar affective disorder. He agrees with admittance to our hospital. Due to severe side effects during treatment with Haldol in the past—tongue protrusion—I decide on therapy with haloperidol.

August 14, 2010

He threatened other patients. Restless, walking around, angry. In the past, verbal aggression has led to physical in similar situations. Physical restraint is needed.
Therapy: idem + Apaurin 5 mg PRN [as needed]

August 15, 2010

After the th. [therapy], Zyprexa VT 20 mg, Apaurin 10 mg, Rivotril 4 mg, the patient sleeps. We're not experiencing apnea signs, but the patient has a weaker swallowing reflex, resulting in coughing. I decide to apply Anexate 1/2 amp i.m. and RF 500 mg ml i.m.

August 16, 2010

Loud, tense. Despite restraints and th., a structured conversation is impossible.
Objective: acutely manic, uncritical, negative, physically aggressive, agitated, risk of violent behavior.
Therapy: Seroquel 2 x 400 mg, Rivotril 3 x 3 mg, Depakine Chrono 2 x 500 mg, Dormicum 15–30 mg PRN

August 19, 2010

The patient is in bed, restrained. He says that we're lying, that he's thankful for our interpretations, and that this whole thing doesn't lead anywhere. After the heteroanamnesis, patient was very restless and tense. In the evening, he needed PRN therapy. He was restrained all the time. During the night, he was supposedly threatening. He received evening therapy in the night when he woke up.
Therapy: Seroquel 2 x 400 mg, Rivotril 3 x 4 mg, Depakine Chrono 2 x 1,000 mg, Dormicum 15–30 mg, Abilify 10, Akineton, Apaurin 1 amp i.m. PRN

August 21, 2010

The patient is in an elevated mood, occasionally loud, psychomotorically agitated, uncritical of his own experience, and negative.
Therapy: idem

August 22, 2010

He is still restrained. Polite in conversation. He says that medication makes him agitated, and his racing thoughts make it hard to control himself. He believes that he can do it. Due to severe extrapyramidal symptoms in the previous hospitalization, the patient is not receiving classical antipsychotics.

Objective: less elevated, not angry; cooperation has improved. He still describes racing thoughts, more critical.

Therapy: Seroquel 2 x 600 mg, the rest as before. Receives Zeldox 1 amp. + Apaurin 1 amp.

Attempt to unrestrain him.

August 24, 2010

The patient's cooperation is orderly, sometimes without distance. After th. PRN sedated, says he feels provocations by others. He understands he's manic.

Objective: better cooperation, still elevated, alluded, partially critical. The risk of violent behavior is still present.

Therapy: Seroquel 2 x 600 mg, Rivotril 3 x 4 mg, Depakine Chrono 2 x 1,000 mg, Dormicum PRN

August 27, 2010

The patient says he's feeling worse than the day before. He woke a patient because he thought there was a standard round and got yelled at. He believes it wasn't his fault, that it wasn't right. He doesn't feel well about it. He realizes it's better to be in the hospital than anywhere else.

He felt good outdoors and asked if he could go for another walk. We agree on solo exits. We plan on transferring him to the open section in a few days.

Objective: lucid, oriented, still elevated, at times incoherent, sped-up, at times still angry, conflictive in a social environment, otherwise participatory, fairly critical in terms of the secured department.

Therapy: Seroquel 2 x 600 mg, Depakine Chrono 2 x 1,000 mg, Rivotril 3 x 3 mg, Dormicum 15–30 mg PRN

August 31, 2010

The patient says he sleeps pretty well and feels good, but he's been avoiding contact with others lately and prefers going to his room. At times he still feels that he's a bit tired. He eats a lot; he noticed that himself. He will try to hold back on food.

Objective: lucid, oriented, formal thinking in order, contently thinking is also stabilizing. The patient is still in an elevated mood but becoming critical about his condition. Nevertheless, he still needs some guidance.

The patient and I agree that he will have a maximum of 10 euros daily at his disposal while in the open section. He will put his bank cards into the safe or give them to his relatives. This agreement will last until the doctor and the patient agree otherwise.

Therapy: Seroquel 2 x 600 mg, Depakine Chrono 2 x 1,000 mg, Apaurin 5-5-7 mg, Dormicum 15–30 mg PRN
Ad E-2 [transfer to the open section]

September 2, 2010

Now calm. He slept for 8 hours.
Therapy: idem

September 5, 2010

In the evening, he returns to the department. In conversation, he states that he wants to sleep at his home. He will return in the morning to discuss his discharge and further treatment. He realizes he's not healthy yet. He believes he's hypomanic. He wants to return to his doctor at Poliklinika.
Objective: structured in conversation, slightly tense, but controls his behavior. Verbally critical of his need for treatment. Denies auto- or hetero-aggressive ideas.
Therapy: idem
He goes home and will return in the morning.

September 6, 2010

He wants to sleep at home again. He realizes he's hypomanic and made a mistake in giving up on medicine. He was taking Quilonorm and decided one day that he wouldn't visit his psychiatrist and wouldn't take medication anymore.
Objective: still in an elevated mood, but he's controlling himself. Verbally critical, not auto- or hetero-aggressive. No disorders in perception or delusional content.
Therapy: idem
Tomorrow he will talk with the section's doctor about further treatment.

September 9, 2010

The patient was admitted to our hospital in a severe manic state, agitated. He had a partial paranoid allusive delusion on admittance but was mostly megalomanic. During the first days of his hospitalization, he was severely agitated with a danger of hetero-aggression. At first, he was mostly verbally aggressive, but restraints were necessary as there was a danger of physical aggression.

After a short period, he reasonably quickly stabilized and was almost euthymic,

calm in the open section.

Today, after a successful weekend at home, we are discharging him.

At discharge, he is euthymic with no contextual thinking disorders. At release, he is critical of his condition. He is reasonably familiar with his psychological state and knows he must take medicine. He promises to attend the checkup 2–3 weeks after the prior arrangement.

* * *

September 21, 2010

The patient is admitted to our hospital for the fifth time. . . .

JAKA TOMC

From Overload to Mania

:):

The first chapter is vital to better understanding mania because of at least three issues. The first is that hypomania can escalate rapidly. I'm talking about hypermania, mania that goes beyond a limit of control. In my case, it usually lasted for a few days. The second issue is delusions. Remember my ideas that I could control the weather and teleport? The third and fundamental issue is overload, or too much of everything at once. It's not recommended for healthy individuals, let alone someone who will walk the line between sanity and craziness for the rest of his life.

In my case, overload was a key trigger for almost every mania. In the first chapter, I wrote about my birthday. Not just any birthday, the thirtieth one. All round numbers are momentous, but thirty is special. It was for me. I can't speak for other people. Besides the preparations for a party of the decade, to which I invited half of Ljubljana, I wanted to publish a book on the same day. Not just any book. In this book, I included a bold line:

This book will explain everything.

I need not explain that I anticipated a lot from that book. Partially my expectations came true, as I've sold all nine hundred printed (and this time perfect-bound) copies. It's been read by many more pairs of eyes, as a free e-book was available online and downloaded by thousands of people. I've received praise from psychiatrists, health-care workers, therapists, medical students, and others. But what matters most is that the book was (and still is) commended by my brothers-in-arms—bipolar people and those close to them. It means more than all the book awards.

I've honored three decades of life on this planet in style with a three-day celebration—the day before, the day itself, and the day after. By now, you already know that the party was a colossal flop, and I realized after a few years that pompous birthday parties are overrated.

Overload isn't necessarily something that starts outside of you. You can as quickly get overloaded with your thoughts. We probably burn out more because of excessive thinking than because of an actual situation. I have. Throughout this book, I will try to present my thoughts during the episodes of mania and depression, but also in remission, or *normal* phase. Let me give you an example so you get a taste of it.

In one of my manic episodes, I was contemplating time. I was pondering that there must exist an infinitely small time unit. Everything can be split into two parts. Take a second. Split it, and you get half a second. Then a quarter, followed by an eighth, and so on. If we continue until the end (I usually did), we reach a point where time stops. Actually, it runs super slowly, but if you observed it in real time, it would appear to stand still because nothing happens in this smallest fragment of time.

Of course, I couldn't stop time, so I thought I could slow it down in a way. I named this process *time expansion*. All I had to do was optimize my actions. That meant I would dress in one minute instead of two, smoke a cigarette in three minutes instead of five, or cross my apartment in four seconds instead of seven. It seems funny, but every day I've gained minutes, maybe even hours of spare time, which I could use in highly productive ways. Sounds great, right? It was a recipe for disaster.

Mania doesn't happen all at once, but you can feel it the minute it arrives if you're attentive and experienced enough. I felt it every time. My cousin once asked me how it felt. I said I started vibrating. The best comparison is the butterflies in your stomach when you're in love. But I feel it all over my body. You can also recognize mania when you open your eyes in the morning. In an interview I did for a Slovene magazine, the journalist went with the title "If You Wake Up Happy in the Morning, You're Already Manic." Nothing wrong with that. I said it. What I meant was that if a bipolar person wakes up in a good mood, but he usually doesn't, it's probably a sign that Auntie Mania has come for a visit. "But that's great," some of you are saying. "If you can feel it, you can beat it." Yes. The critical question isn't *can you* beat it? It's do you *want* to?

Why would anyone want to be manic? It's a legitimate question. The answer is simple. It's beautiful. If you're recovering from a severe depression that lasted for months, you will grab that morning smile on your face and lock it somewhere safe. Hypomania is wonderful. You love the world around you again. You love yourself. The colors are bright again. The food tastes right. You can speak. You can read a book. You're not scared anymore. Are you sure you wouldn't take a pill that would make those things happen if someone offered it to you? I took it every time, even though I promised myself I wouldn't. Suffering versus Life. Fear versus Love. Misery versus Beauty. Those are just a few examples.

In reality, the gap between depression and mania is a lot wider. That's why they invented the middle ground. The purgatory. Walking the line. *Remission* is a lovely word for the temporary disappearance of the symptoms of the disease. We could also call it a standstill. Because that's precisely what it is—no depressions, no manias, at least not the big ones.

But there's another thing about remission that should be mentioned. Between a plus and a minus, there's precisely one number: zero.

Waking Up with a Smile

:):

As far as my experience with mania goes, if I take away the first one I couldn't prepare for, I always wanted to be manic. I'm talking about hypomania, a mild mania that can be tamed. If it were up to me, I'd make everyone hypomanic. Especially people who steer through life in search of happiness. I once wrote that mania is the problematic sister of depression. I was talking about hypermania, a severe mania that is practically uncontrollable. In my case, it was mixed with delusions, fears, and sometimes aggression. Because hypermania lasts for a short period, especially if they have to hospitalize you, I will talk about hypomania from now on and call it mania, even though it would deserve a nicer name.

To understand mania, we need to know a few things about depression. I'll talk about that later, so let's discuss its antipode. I could say that mania is terrific and be done with it. But it's a lot more than that.

It always started with a smile. When I opened my eyes in the morning, something was different, as if someone had taken all the burdens that life had bestowed upon me. Of course, not all at once, but enough that getting out of bed in the morning was different than the day before. It was the smile that replaces a sigh. I know you know what I mean. When you wake up two minutes before the alarm goes off, but you hope it's the middle of the night. When you're depressed, every morning is like that. Your bed is a haven you don't want to leave, except in case of a natural disaster. That's why that smile is so unusual and so pleasing. I can't describe the feelings that overwhelmed me when it happened. It's morning. The same as every morning before it, but you've changed. The stuff that bothered you in the evening is still there, but the problems seem smaller and easier to overcome, and you know they are solvable. That smile turns into the first morning coffee, and it tastes right again. Silence turns into music, colors overrun shades of gray, and emptiness is filled with a whole spectrum of emotions. The intensity depends on how long you've wandered the infinite abyss of melancholia. You're craving feelings, and when that morning smile arrives, you grab it with both hands and hope it's not a one-hit wonder.

Then it begins. Butterflies in the gut. A tingling sensation all over your body. You need to talk to people. Hang out with them. You don't need to sleep so much. Fresh ideas appear out of thin air. They might be business ideas or big life decisions, or you need new things. Spending money over one's financial abilities clearly indicates someone is manic. I'm talking about people with diagnoses. Otherwise, someone might think half the population of Slovenia is manic.

As I've said before, the problem is not that I wouldn't feel mania as it prepared to take control over my brain. It's as if I—and this is very important—let it take control. I remember when I first said that I didn't want to hear about mania anymore and that it was my last time riding that roller coaster. Soon came new episodes and, with them, new hospitalizations. I didn't care about it while I was manic. It would be like rich folks worrying about having money and trying to get rid of it. Every single time, I thought I had complete control and could overcome mania with no consequences. If I ever do, I'll share the recipe with you. Until then, I'm trying to stay clear of mania.

Mania is like a drug. When it's in your body, it's beautiful. What kind of drug? Excellent question. Judging by the ones I've tried, it's a mixture of cocaine and MDMA (ecstasy). You have a copious amount of energy, and you love (almost) everybody. You can talk to anyone about everything. You have loads of ideas that mostly stay in the metaphysical realm as new ones appear while you're analyzing one of them. The most bizarre thing in my case was that every time the mania came, I was convinced that I could write spectacularly. Best-selling books. Song lyrics that bands wouldn't be able to refuse. Blog posts that thousands in Slovenia would read and maybe even millions all over the globe. Why bizarre? Because I haven't written anything worth mentioning. Nothing I would be proud of. I did write a blog post titled "I Like You, but No Sex Tonight." You won't find it anywhere, as I was able to delete it from the intestines of the Internet. No novels, no novellas, no short stories. Too much time was spent on new ideas, too little on realizing them. Or, as a wise man said: "Jaka, there are millions of ideas, but until you materialize one of them, they're completely worthless."

While manic, checking if one's still in one's body is imperative. Forget about soul, aura, energy bodies, and other New Age terms. You don't have to believe it, but you can believe me and my decade-and-a-half-long experience with mania. When I'm talking about not being present in my body, I mean the feeling of absence. It's like you're not centered. Even when I'm "in my head," I say I'm out of my body. When I was manic, I wasn't just in my head. I was all over the place. On regular days I think a lot. My manic brain is working in overdrive. I once wrote that I can see, hear, and feel more. It's an absolute truth. A manic person's brain is lit like a Christmas tree. Precisely that part of mania, my ability to think more broadly and profoundly, was so tempting that I couldn't resist it. But, similar to writing, nothing much came out of the hyperactive thought process. Except for interesting conversations with strangers. One time I managed to draw my ideas on a blackboard. I tried to explain the drawing to someone days after, but with no success. I'm not very good at drawing.

Even though I suspect it's the law of attraction, I'm not sure why everything seems to work out fine when you're manic. Because you're positive, you attract positive people. Because you're aware, you notice positive things. Because you're outgoing and have a surplus of energy, you spread that energy to others. You *live* life, and the universe provides. I've met incredible people during my manias. I have found myself in pleasant situations. Unpleasant too, but I reacted differently than I would now. Or I wouldn't end up in them in the first place. Everything is simple when you're manic. Running through possible scenarios is pushed to the background. You decide intuitively and instinctively. You wholeheartedly trust yourself because you love yourself immensely. When you love yourself, you can love others.

If I had to describe mania in one sentence, I'd do it like this. In mania, you dare to be who you are. Period. It's similar to people when they're drunk. Everything that's repressed bursts out. That's why I assume that if you're a jerk and you pretend you're not in everyday life, you'll just be a manic (or drunk) jerk. When I was severely manic, a lot of repressed stuff erupted. Aggression, paranoia, even xenophobia and racism. "Oh, so you're a racist, pretending not to be one!" Maybe. Or maybe I carry patterns of my ancestors, just like we all do. Some people think that's just mumbo-jumbo, even though it's basic biology and genetics. I'm pretty sure I'm not a racist, and I'm confident I'm not an aggressive human being, but I still choked my father during an argument while I was hypermanic. What's also true is that I have a lot of repressed anger, and severe manias tend to bring it out of me. Anger and fears. You do know where fears lead, right? If you're not a *Star Wars* fan, this will probably be the first time you hear it. Fear leads to anger, anger leads to hate, hate leads to suffering, and suffering leads to the Dark Side. You don't have to be a science fiction enthusiast to find these words by Master Yoda an utter and unquestionable truth.

JAKA TOMC

Mom's Chapter

:):

It was just another hot late-summer day. The sun was beating down like it was trying to show everything it was capable of. It was capable of a lot.

Jaka and I were supposed to meet at his apartment, but he texted me he'd be waiting for me at the station. I wasn't exactly thrilled about it; just the opposite. I was afraid of wandering the sunbaked streets, constant changes of direction, and sudden decisions about our next destination.

He was already waiting for me when I arrived at the Ljubljana bus station. My child. My son. My everything.

He wore a white T-shirt with something printed on the front, brown and dark green slacks, flip-flops, and a straw hat. I hugged him, and he hugged me back absentmindedly. Not a second had passed, and he was already in motion. We were walking quite fast down Miklosiceva Street toward the city center. I was doing most of the talking about work, home, news of the day. I had a feeling he wasn't listening. He just walked, and I walked with him, sometimes behind him, sometimes in front. We stopped at Čokl, a café near his home.

Thank God, *I thought.* We'll drink a cup of coffee and go to his place. He'll be safe there, far from hot asphalt, rushing people, and everything that could agitate him.

Things didn't go according to plan. We were in the same place the whole afternoon. Well, at least I was. Jaka was coming and going. He sat briefly, said a few words, brought something to me, then rushed away again. For a while now, he couldn't stay in one place. He couldn't find peace anywhere.

The afternoon soon became evening. It was half past seven. In forty-five minutes, the last train would depart. Jaka didn't want me to escort him to his home. He suggested he walk with me to the station. It was hard for me to leave, as he didn't look well. We said goodbye at the station. He let me hug him. He was somehow uptight and strange but also helpless and vulnerable. I wanted to stay with him but couldn't say it aloud. I watched as he walked away with his head down, into the sunset.

I was staring at nothing on the train. There was a lump in my throat, and my heart was crying. But there wasn't a single tear in my eyes. My tears were long gone. I just wanted to get home as soon as possible, lie in bed, and leave everything behind me.

I wanted to wake up in a new morning and in a place where my child would be happy again. Well, maybe tomorrow will be that Tomorrow.

There's Always a First Time

:):

When you experience it for the first time, you have no idea what's going on. Almost everyone has experienced short-term depression—the kind that lasts for a few hours or days. It's part of life and absolutely normal. But when depression extends to weeks or even months, alarms must go off, and we need to act.

I encountered my first severe depression at the beginning of 2007, after my girlfriend of almost five years broke up with me. I was unstable before that, but after the phone conversation, of which I remember only her words "I want to be with someone else," I was thrown into the abyss. Not immediately, but after a few days, when the initial shock ended. Things tend to go downhill when you talk to someone about living together and picking the furniture, and then about packing your stuff a few days later. Today I'm glad it happened. We're both happy with our own families. We were exhausting ourselves in our relationship, we weren't compatible, and we (as many couples do) tried to save what wasn't meant to be until it snapped. The only problem was that she found refuge in another person's embrace while I found shelter in an infinitely dark place.

Somebody advised me to move at once. Throw my things in the car and drive away. I listened to him. I loaded my clothes and other stuff in the back of my car, put my keys on the cabinet, and left for good. Actually, we met one more time because I wanted closure, but it didn't quite go as I expected. She literally ran out of the bar, into her car, and drove away. I tried to catch her with my car but gave up after five minutes. The worst closure ever. But they can't all be good. With a car full of my things (luckily I had a car with more trunk space then), I returned home to my parents. If you've ever done that after a few years of living somewhere else, you know what I'm talking about, so I won't discuss it further. I was twenty-six, and living with my parents at that age was nothing unusual or shameful. But returning to my eight-square-meter room full of childhood memories was a horrible defeat. It wasn't doing any good for my mood either. I slowly spilled over the edge and fell into the dark pit.

If you wake up with a smile during mania, depression mornings usually start with a desperate sigh or a curse. If you jump out of bed in mania because you want to live your day to the fullest, depression pins you down on the bed.
If you're lucky, you have a job and an office to go to. If you don't, you can lie in bed or on the couch for days, taking only toilet and (if you haven't lost your appetite) fridge breaks.

Sometimes someone asks you to meet for coffee because he wants to do something for you. These coffees can do more harm than good. In my case, they often ended with a panic attack that usually began with the idea that everyone in the bar was looking at me and knowing that something was wrong with me. The fact that the person who got you in this mess is talking while you're nodding or giving one-word comments isn't helping either. Of course, it all depends on the stage of depression you're in. When you're at the bottom, you can't socialize, especially with strangers. Going for a walk with a friend who understands your need for silence is a good idea. Writing emails is too. In any case, don't force people dealing with depression into activities they don't like. No matter how much you love them. We can deal with certain things only by ourselves, and confronting our demons (depression being a colossal demon) is at the top of the list.

I was one of the lucky ones. I had a job where I had to pretend I was okay. Another stroke of luck was that it was the beginning of the year, and I had to prepare an annual report for the European Commission on my project. When I was almost drowning in sweat and tears, my coworkers advised me not to overthink the task. They said I should assemble whatever I'd done and send it. Unfortunately, the perfectionist in me was conscious enough, so I tried to deliver the best report in the history of the European Union. Perfectionism and depression don't go well together; I can tell you that.

My depression was soon joined by insomnia. I was contemplating the report and other work stuff at night. For the first time, I felt my brain working. It felt like it was made of little wheels that could turn into infinity. I slept only a few hours a night. I was waking up at three or four in the morning. I think it lasted for about three weeks—maybe more. During the day, I was spaced out due to lack of sleep, so I took my work home and worked in the evenings and early mornings. My daily routine collapsed and built itself in a new way, but it didn't work. Because of insomnia and the submission deadline getting close, my stress level was going through the roof. That period was probably the hardest in my life. I was falling apart.

When you're depressed, you have much time to think about your past, present, and future. You can't think about anything other than yourself. But because you're in a dark mood, your self-reflection and introspection are very distorted. You're convinced that you're not good at anything, you're ugly, your past is a disaster, and the future holds nothing good for you. Your lifetime achievements are irrelevant. Even if you still believe you possess some skills, they're worthless, and you cannot make the world a better place. You're a drop lost in the vast ocean, and it's your fault. If your life were a building, it would fall apart before your eyes, with one crucial detail—you observe the whole process from within. That particular moment, when the building is about to fall and crush you, is vital. Too many people decide that they will not wait for the outcome and choose the emergency exit. Luckily, I never did.

Why is the collapse of the building so important? Because it gives you precisely three options. The first one I already mentioned is the emergency exit, or suicide. The second one is leaving the building through the main entrance because you decide things can't go on like this, and you need to do something for them to change. Behind door number three is probably the most painful option but also the most liberating—you watch the building collapse on itself. In this case, I've used the metaphor of a crumbling building, but I'm usually talking about falling to the ground. When you're in the midst of ruins, you've hit rock bottom. When you're at the bottom, there's only one way that remains, and it leads upward.

During my first depression, I didn't reach the bottom—probably one of the ledges in the wall, but not the lowest point. But I do know what made the curve change its course. Ice cream and *Big Brother*.
I know it sounds silly, but that's how it was. *Big Brother* could've been any other TV show, but at that particular moment, it was what I needed. I was desperate for a show that enabled me to turn off my brain and that had people in it who were not perfect. If there's one thing you don't need when you're depressed, it's perfect (or perfect on the outside) people. You don't need people who easily cruise through life, because you're intentionally or unintentionally comparing yourself to them whenever you end up short. When you're depressed, you're a Yugo; the last thing you need is to be surrounded by Maseratis. Fords, Alfa Romeos, Fiats, and Volkswagens are the types of people you want close to you and who are beneficial for your health.

That's why I enjoyed the reality show that was all but a show. But at least it was real. I ate a liter of ice cream every evening while watching Fords and Fiats doing their thing. Week after week, I was regaining my strength.

I felt alive again. I was braver. I was still a Yugo, but I made peace with myself. I was physically active again. I often went running while listening to some fine tunes. The report that I worked on until the final deadline found its way to Brussels. My life made sense again, and I wanted to try something new. Soon I moved to an apartment in Prule, Ljubljana. For the first time in my life, I became a tenant. I was single, I was a depression survivor, and I had the whole apartment available for new adventures.

The manic odyssey that would last for six months had begun, and it ended epically, with my first hospitalization.

Crazy, Crazier, Madhouse

:):

My first mania happened about a year before, but in December 2007, it was so severe that there was no other way but to hospitalize me. A lot was going on that year. In the summer, I drove to Paris by myself. I had decided to go a few days prior. It's not entirely unusual, but when I remember that week, I know I was at least slightly manic. Luckily not too much, otherwise who knows what would've been the outcome of my episode at a strip club on Pigalle where I left owing two hundred euros. I had no clue that a bottle of champagne (probably just some cheap sparkling wine; I was drinking beer) and a lap dance by a petite stripper named Mimi cost three hundred euros. I was sure a hundred-euro bill in my wallet would easily suffice. Especially after a guy at the entrance guaranteed that the entrance fee, which was ten euros, entitled me to watch and have a free drink. You can't know those things when you're twenty-seven and have no mileage in Slovene strip clubs. So they took me outside. To a dingy alley. Two gorillas and me. I'd leave the rest of the story to your vivid imagination, as the truth is much less captivating. They took me to an improvised cashier's desk. I knew I had no money in my account, and my credit card was maxed. I still tried, though. It wouldn't have been the first time money magically appeared in my bank account. That night it didn't. I agreed with the goons that I'd pay a hundred and bring the rest the next day. I never did. But I did leave Paris in the afternoon. My mother had to wire me some money so I could buy gas and some food. What is the point of the strip club story? Am I trying to brag that I had too much money? Or that I was bored? Maybe both? No. When you're manic, things align in the right places and for your benefit.

When I returned from Paris, I met some of my former work colleagues at Bailey's, another legendary place in Ljubljana that's now drowned in oblivion. The first bottle of sparkling wine appeared on our table, followed quickly by a second one. I'm almost sure we also drank some spirits. I have a vivid memory of the boisterous waiter and flying glasses. We closed the bar and moved on. We spent the night at someone's apartment and headed to the city with the first rays of sunlight. We continued our invigorating debates over a cup of coffee that soon evolved into rounds of beer. Somebody suggested that we go swimming in the Ljubljanica River. The decision was unanimous. During the short walk, I jumped into the fountain on Breg and swam a full circle. The Ljubljanica swim was not so special. The river was cold and full of algae. But I can proudly tell a story about a few guys who heroically jumped into water that is not meant for bathing.

There were some other things I did in the coming years that I wouldn't have done if I hadn't been manic.

That summer, I met an acquaintance from the time I was bowling. Together we found a place in Zalog and moved in. The semi-basement apartment was nothing special, but I transformed some sort of winter garden into my room. The space was meant for growing plants and drying the laundry, not for human habitation. The quality of living was questionable, but I didn't care about humidity and low temperature. At that moment, the wildest period of my life began. We attended almost all mentionable events in Ljubljana. In just a few months, I met more people than in my whole life up to that point. Wednesdays, Thursdays, Fridays, and Saturdays were our party days. I'm not sure what kept me on the ground during those times. Maybe alcohol. Maybe the fact that I didn't bother thinking about where I was heading. I simply let go and enjoyed the moments. Until it all started falling apart like a poorly built house of cards. . . .

One day, I believe it was in October 2007, I quit my job. I wasn't a writer then, at least not the kind who's writing books. I was a mediocre journalist, writing simple articles and recording short videos. I'm not saying journalism is easy, because it's not. *I* took the easy path with almost no ambitions of becoming an established journalist. That's why I've never seen myself as a journalist, even after years of working for different media. Even today, I seldom use that word, except when I don't feel like explaining what I was doing.

The job I quit was at a public company running EU projects. A considerable burden fell off my back.

Working there exhausted me. Not because it was too hard. For half a year, I was working depressed. I had no idea then what was going on with me. Someone "diagnosed" me with burnout, and she might have been right. Looking back, I know it was depression that may have led to burnout because I was trying too hard to do my job well (and struggling to fake that I was okay).

What happens when the curve bends upward? You ride it and fly, thrilled that the suffering is over, at least for a while. Ljubljana happened, Poreč happened, Paris happened, London happened. Mania happened in its purest form. Life was beautiful, and I was invincible. I felt like a child again. Who wouldn't want that?

That year, 2007, was a landmark for me and my health. I started smoking at twenty-seven. I had smoked a cigarette once in a while before, but that summer evening in Poreč, Croatia, I bought my first pack of smokes and decided that I was going to be a smoker. If I didn't truly start then, I started in earnest half a year later when I was taken to a psychiatric institution for the first time.

I have numerous memories of the autumn/winter of 2007. Some of them are nice, some of them not so much. Most memories are tangled in my brain like a giant Gordian knot. Luckily I have thousands of photos that remind me of dozens of parties we attended. I bought myself an excellent camera, not because I had too much money but because I desired it. When you're manic, you don't complicate your use of cash. If you have it, you spend it.

If you don't, you find a way. I usually took a certain amount of money when I went out, and then I took care that I emptied my wallet. The next day I repeated the drill. I borrowed money only from my mother. In most cases, those were loans I didn't repay.

It happened around Christmas. On Christmas Eve, I was so manic I was all over the place. Everybody was with their families, but I argued with my parents and decided I would spend Christmas Eve alone. What could go wrong? At a particular moment, I was chatting with somebody on the computer when I suddenly realized they were surveilling me. I grabbed the cell phone and dropped it into a full coffee mug. There were no smartphones then, so I imagined a listening device inside the phone. It made sense. I don't know why I didn't go to my grandma's place, two hundred meters away. Maybe I did. Perhaps I argued with her as well. Christmas Eve, and I was all alone and paranoid—a perfect combination.

I somehow survived the night and chatted with a friend the following day. This is a genuine transcript (translated into English), and you can see clearly what a chat with a manic person looks like.

December 25, 2007

XY: *when are we meeting at ***?*
06:51 **me**: *I hope today*
    that's what he said
    or is he messing with us again

once it's Christmas, once New Year
hes so confused
then he calls me if I have a pot
beh
he gave it to me for fruit trontlje
06:52 **me**: *fruit, yes*
I'm typing too fast
damn, I forgot about the ice
wait
06:59 **me**: *I'm back*
XY: *ok*
07:03 **me**: *do you have any idea when *** waks up*
07:04 **XY**: *no*
unfortunately no
me: *eh*
do you know where she is?
07:05 *please tell me*
I wanna help her
XY: *with what?*
me: *I knew you were gonna say that*
XY: *I have no idea where she is. How am I supposed to know?*
me: *you knoe*
I don't know
mah...she'll help herself
or?
07:06 **XY**: *I have no idea*
I don't even know what she needs help with.
07:07 **me**: *yeah*
I know
I already made the arrangement

thx
*07:10 **XY**: what arrangement?*
*07:11 **me**: how we're meeting*
or what
never mind
I texted her

In my next memory, which is very strong and clear, I'm lying in bed, taking a nap. When I checked the time, it was six. Nothing unusual. But at that moment, I had no idea if it was six in the morning or six in the evening. My mind overflowed. The ground was pulled out from under my feet, even if I was lying down. My roommate and his friend who was joining us at most parties burst into my room. I imagine they wanted to say hi, but I saw the situation differently. I was sure they wanted to hurt me or call somebody who would do it. I shat myself, but mostly I felt betrayed. And not for the last time that evening . . .

First, we went to the ER so they could fix my broken foot. Wait a minute, when did you break your foot? I'd tell you if I knew. I suspect it was in London a few days before, but it could have been anywhere, anytime. I walked for as long as I could. When the pain became debilitating, I limped. Walk it off, Jaka. Unfortunately, the foot didn't heal, so I got a cast—the first one in my life. I told you it was a special year. They didn't take me home from the ER. Looking at that night now, I'm positive my family and friends made the right decision. But at that time, it was the biggest betrayal possible.

JAKA TOMC

We were standing in front of the psychiatric hospital known as Polje: me, my former best friend, my former roommate, my mother, and my uncle. I told them repeatedly that I needed a good night's sleep. I know now that I was partly correct, but I probably wouldn't have slept much with such severe mania. I tried to run away, over the fields toward my apartment, with one leg in a cast. I didn't get far, so I accepted my destiny.

It was what it was at the reception office, but it indeed wasn't good, or I would have spent that night in my own bed. What I mean is that the doctor-on-call decided that I was to spend at least one night at their place. We went to the higher ground floor, where the reception ward is, also known as a closed ward. My people were by my side. I asked them to walk with me all the way. But they couldn't. Not there. The door closed, and I was left all alone. In terrible despair, I grabbed the keys from a doctor's hand. I remember standing in the unknown hallway, scared to death, while a group of strange people was closing in on me. Of course, the medical technicians grabbed me, and a few minutes later I was strapped and sedated in bed. I got another medical record and a case number that would accompany me through my hospitalizations in the years to come. In the final breaths of 2007, I became number 829.

December 2007/ January 2008

:):

December 27, 2007

The patient is admitted to our clinic for the first time. The Service for Urgent Medical Help referred him with a referral diagnosis: Aggravated psychosis.

At admittance, the on-call doctor notes:

"Who are you? A doctor? Who can I believe? These friends? Are they even my friends? Yes, I feel like a puppet. Who? You? Are you my girlfriend? What do you want from me? Who am I? Am I even me?"

Hetero-anamnesis:

His uncle, mother, and friends tell me that he joined a meditation group two years ago. He said that his chakras had fallen to pieces. It lasted for a few days. In the summer, he started to drink alcohol excessively. He was rude and changed.

He started acting weird again last week. They did nothing right, and he began accusing them of several things. He said that somebody was walking around his apartment.

At night he didn't sleep but walked around, taking photographs.

He complained that they made rules for him. He spoke incoherently and without making any sense.

When they were in London, he hurt his leg. That's why they were in the ER today (he has a walking cast).

He didn't take drugs, except two weeks ago when he smoked a joint with a friend.

He visited a psychiatrist this year after a breakup with his girlfriend. He said he was depressed. He took medication, but they don't know which one.

Psychological status:
Clear conscience, but he can't connect to an orderly conversation. Weak associations, the ductus is dissociated—he's mistrusting, tense, and remote. He seems to act under productive psychopathologic symptomatic [hallucinations] influence. Indications of depersonalization and derealization disorders. He refuses to be hospitalized.

Judging by the hetero-anamnesis, the patient suffers from a psychotic experience.

Somatic and neurological status:
Unaffected. Without peculiarities.

Medical opinion:
The patient is acutely psychotic. He is a danger to himself, and his life is at risk. We admit him to a secure department against his will.
Obstruction and therapy are necessary.

Nursing opinion:

The patient is tense, suspicious, and negative. He was accompanied to our department by staff and then obstructed.

December 28, 2007

Since he started meditating, something began to change inside him. During one of the workshops, he lost consciousness. Yesterday, when admitted, he was panicking. He doesn't know why. He feels like he doesn't know anybody anymore. He isn't sure if they changed. The last few days were weird. Everybody weirdly misunderstands him. He felt threatened if his friend had done the opposite of what he told him. He doesn't know what scared him at the ER. He doesn't hear voices. He hasn't noticed that people changed concerning him. He smoked pot two weeks ago.

Clinically appropriate in relation. He seems confused and somewhat tense. Emotionally diverse, responsive. Losing focus now and then. The thought ductus is a bit loose. He mentions feelings of unclear change of environment, irrational reactions of the people he knows, and paranoia. He denies disorders in his sensory spectrum.

Th.: Abilify 10+0+0 mg

December 31, 2007

He feels better. He's wondering if he has to be at the hospital. His fear during the admission felt like a fear of the situation. He doesn't resent his friends for bringing him here.

He asks himself who told us that he was sleeping less than before.

Clinically talkative. He tries to show himself as more relaxed than he is. Still a bit tense and suspicious. Thoughts formally in order. Substantively no productive symptoms were detected.

Th.: Abilify 25+0+0 mg, Loram 3 x 1.25 mg
Ad I-2 department [transferred to the open ward]

January 3, 2008

Auto-anamnesis:
He came here because his family thought something was going on with him. He was brought here by two of his friends. The situation was the same as the year before. He was working on a European project. Burnout happened as he was working too much. He went to a psychiatrist and visited her a few times, but it didn't seem necessary anymore. Until October 2007, things were a little calmer at work. He still worked on a European project. Then he stopped working there and got a job as a journalist at Dnevnik newspaper. His workload was more immense again. He worked from nine in the morning to midnight. He felt like he was losing his grip on reality. He saw and heard things. He believed things were happening because of him. He called the psychiatrist he visited a year before, and she gave him a date for group therapy, January 15, 2008. A week before the admission, he was in London as a tourist with a friend. These "weird thoughts" appeared when he came back from London. He was at home then. He's practicing Reiki and aromatherapy. He lives with a friend as a tenant. His family consists of his

parents, a grandmother, two uncles, and an aunt. His mother is an accountant, and his father is an electrician.

Childhood and youth:
As a child, he was calm. He played alone a lot. He learned to read when he was three years old. He went to kindergarten. He started primary school at age seven. He should have skipped the first class, but in the school psychologist's opinion, he was "too childish." He was an excellent pupil and had good relationships with other pupils. He went to a secondary school and finished it with middle grades. He earned a bachelor's in human resource management from the Faculty of Social Sciences. At first, he worked at the National Radio and Television, then at Dnevnik newspaper, then on European projects. Two years ago, he started meditating with his girlfriend, who broke up with him after a five-year relationship.

Family anamnesis:
His grandfather had cancer; his grandmother has diabetes. As a child, he had a minor concussion once.
In his free time, he meditates, reads, writes prose and poetry, takes photos, cooks, and loves to travel. He smokes a few cigarettes per day. Occasionally he smokes pot.

Conclusion:
The twenty-seven-year-old patient was admitted to our hospital for the first time with the initial diagnosis of aggravated psychosis. At the patient's request, we're dismissing him after one week. There is no reason to keep him here against his will.

The patient has taken psychological tests.

At dismissal, the patient's perception is clear, but his thoughts occasionally wander. Ductus is fluid and coherent. He denies productive psychopathological symptoms. Emotionally adequately diverse, middle mood position. He denies suicidal thoughts. Critical.

I advise against drinking alcohol and smoking pot. I suggest liver tests. We also recommend a head CT to rule out organic causes of the disorder.

Dismissal therapy: Abilify 30 mg in the morning

* * *

January 5, 2008

A gentleman is admitted to our clinic for the second time. . . .

Bent but Not Broken

:):

I vividly remember the reason for my second hospitalization, which happened just two days after they dismissed me. We were at my grandma's when suddenly my arm started to bend. Arms tend to bend, but mine bent unnaturally. It looked like a scene from a horror movie. We promptly got in the car and raced back to the hospital. The situation was getting worse. The closer we were to our destination, the more my arm was bent. I thought it would break, so I opened the car door. My father, who was driving, yelled at me to shut it, and I cried back that I couldn't take it anymore. When we finally made it to the hospital and got out of the car, my neck tightened. This is what the hospital staff wrote at admission:

He is petrified, compulsory posture of the neck (looking sideways) and left arm (he's holding it away from the body, turned inside at the wrist). Tonus is not elevated. We can passively move the arm. Then he returns it to the previous position. He denies sensory dysfunction. He confirms he is very scared.

They probably gave me a strong sedative when I was taken to the closed ward. I remember lying on the floor while other patients gathered around me. I have no idea how long

I was down, but I don't think it was too long. I suddenly stood up and marched to my room. They didn't strap me to the bed. There was no reason to.

I was in the hospital for ten days. Besides having my cast taken off, I don't remember a thing. At discharge, I got an appointment for a head CT scan. But that wasn't the end. They did another thing. They rolled a snowball down the hill that quickly became an avalanche. When it hit me, it paralyzed me for quite some time.

Bad Memory

:):

Because I'm not supposed to cruise through life effortlessly, I got another diagnosis in 2008—brain atrophy. I was diagnosed with it during severe depression. When CT of my head showed initial atrophy of the cerebellum and cerebral cortex, my world was suddenly shattered. I imagined a near future in which I couldn't walk and talk anymore. I demanded additional tests, and they sent me to a neurologist at the psychiatric clinic.

When I arrived, another surprise was waiting for me in the form of medical students. I'm not sure if it's luck or a curse, but the students are there almost every time I'm in a hospital or at a medical checkup. Nothing wrong with that. They need to learn somewhere and from someone. But why always me?

My memory is terrible, but I can vividly remember the beginning of the conversation with the neurologist.

"Can you tell me why you are here?"

"My memory is not working correctly."

"What do you want to remember?"

What do I want to remember? The question blew me away. "Everything!" I yelled in my head. Events, conversations, and things I was scared were lost forever. One of my friends once said her first memory was from the womb. Yes, you read that correctly. She remembers things that happened before she was born. I couldn't even remember the conversation on the phone that took place a few hours ago.

The students and I got an assignment. They had to tell me a few sayings, and I had to explain them the best I could. Have you ever tried to explain an expression? A healthy person can have trouble with it, let alone a depressed guy with a newly diagnosed brain atrophy. My explanations were fundamental. "If it glitters, it's not necessarily gold." The student choir was having fun. I wasn't. Not one bit. They started competing amongst themselves to see which one would put the best saying on the table. If I couldn't decipher the evergreen *All that glitters isn't gold*, how was I supposed to explain *In the land of the blind, the one-eyed man is king?* The final result was Students 6, Jaka 0.

The sayings were followed by repeating numbers and names. I was very good at that. Then I had to pretend I was combing my hair and brushing my teeth. I aced it.
The neurologist concluded I don't have the ability of abstract thinking. Otherwise, I'm fine. Fine? My brain was dying, and he thought I was fine. He tried to calm me down. It wasn't a big deal. He said he knows a man with brain atrophy who's a world-class mathematician. The brain is a complex organ, and other healthy parts take over the function of the parts that die. At least, that was what my doctor said.

Fifteen years have passed since I visited the neurologist, and I have no idea what's happening with my atrophy. It could be better or worse, but nothing will change if I know the current situation. I try to live day by day. I know my memory is terrible, but I've gotten used to it. The COVID pandemic and my father's death made me think about my mortality. If my psychiatrist hadn't changed my therapy, I might have forgotten I was bipolar. I'm trying to say that diagnoses are diagnoses, and life, as much as we have left of it, is what we make it. Live every day like it's your last.

JAKA TOMC

Neurologist's Diagnosis

:):

June 2, 2008

A twenty-eight-year-old journalist comes to the checkup because he can't remember things. He says he feels he forgets all recent and distant events. He says that he usually can't remember what he did or said. He states that he had a lower concentration level since he was very young. Good space orientation. Last December, he had an episode of changed experience of the people close to him. At times he was sadder and crying. In the fall, he changed his job, a year before his girlfriend broke up with him after many years. Since December, he has been more hyperactive at work and in his personal life. He sleeps less. He doesn't fulfill his duties as before. During the diagnosis treatment, he underwent a head CT showing more expansive subarachnoid liquor spaces of the gyri creases of both frontal and parietal lobes, initial cortical atrophy, and cerebellum atrophy.

Four years ago, he had a red stain on the abdomen skin. After antibiotic treatment, it cleared up. Twenty-two years ago, he sustained head trauma without losing consciousness. He has a bachelor's degree in sociology.
He smokes and drinks alcohol occasionally and moderately. In December, he smoked pot for a few weeks, no more than ten joints. He took ecstasy once.

He denies allergies to medications. He doesn't have any medicines. In his family, there have been no known neurological diseases that would result in forgetfulness.

Indifferent, attentive. He repeats the correct sequence of at least six numbers, and in reversed order of at least five. His speech is clear, fluid, and makes sense. He repeats correctly. He understands speech reasonably. I can find no impairment in memory capabilities. I also can't find impairment in functional abilities. I can confirm a disturbance in abstract thinking. Today: Short Test of Functional Capabilities 30/30, Clock Drawing Test 4/4. Neurological status, including examination of the head, neck, limbs, sensibility, standing and walking coordination, and frontal tests, no abnormalities.

Conclusion:

Today's neurological exam shows no convincing downfall of mental capabilities or other loss of the nervous system—discretely disturbed abstract thinking but in no case dementia. Due to a slightly enigmatic head CT, I suggest psychological testing and a head MRI by the judgment of his treating psychiatrist. If not, we could only decide on clinical observation and further diagnostic treatment in case of deterioration.

I Trade My Intelligence for Inner Peace

:):

During an interview for an online magazine, a friend asked me if I consider myself to be of above-average intelligence. Maybe even a genius. My answer was:

The only intelligence test I've ever done was during the testing for military service. I never got the results and didn't work for military intelligence. I'm not a genius. I'm just a human who dared to look deeper into himself and face his fears. If that makes me above average, so be it.

I knew where he was aiming with that question. Many brilliant people are dealing with mental illnesses, one being bipolar disorder. I believe there is a connection between high intelligence and mental illnesses. Not because I want to elevate myself. I'll try to say it without hurting anyone. Some of us are more observant of our inner and outer world and are consequently more susceptible to mental health issues. I've said it many times and sometimes meant it: I would trade my high IQ for normality and life without bothering about stuff I can do nothing about.

Every time somebody sends me a list of famous people with bipolar disorder, I barely throw a glance. I am who I am, and rarely if ever do I compare myself to famous people. Of course, I'd love to be celebrated as Stephen King is (he's not bipolar, at least not officially, but he had a history of alcohol and drug abuse), but that doesn't mean that I'll become a best-selling author. Speaking of authors, I stumbled upon research that was done in the '80s. For several years scientists observed thirty renowned British writers. Eighty percent had some sort of mood disorder. Forty-three percent of them were bipolar, and thirty percent were alcoholics. If you don't want trouble with mental illnesses, stay away from writing. . . .

When answering my friend's question, I inadvertently lied. I forgot that I had taken another intelligence test. When they put you through numerous tests, some might slip your mind. On May 27, 2008, they measured my IQ, which was 127. Considering I was depressed during the trial, I dare to argue I could do better.

The patient looks tidy and pleasant in contact. He establishes a social connection appropriately. In conversation, he is cooperative and talkative. Thinking is coherent and logically connected. The emotional response is adequate.
He approaches the test assignments adequately motivated.
The exhibited mental capabilities are highly above average (CIQ = 127). No impairment of individual functions has been detected.
The profile shows a person who tends to walk away

from a social situation and is unsociable, nontrusting, and nonaccepting. He strives for stability and certainty. He has difficulties adapting to new life situations. He tends to be organized. He could be pedantic and thorough. He is cautious, anxious, and worried. He is discontented with life perspectives. He feels deprived, left out, and lonely. He is often sad and miserable. Critical about other people. He's prone to arguing and proving himself.

MMPI [Minnesota Multiphasic Personality Inventory]: 201
Conflict in family relationships is implied. Trouble with identifying and expressing emotions. Defiance, egocentricity, proneness to denial of psychological issues.

Rorschach Test
The protocol doesn't deviate fundamentally from the average. Thinking is productive and efficient, socially adequately adapted. The ability to observe and concentrate is high. The emotional response is outwardly adequate and appropriately in control. Introspection into his emotional reaction is worse. The interest in the social environment is preserved, but the relations are marked with anxiety.
The contact with reality is adequate.

Conclusion:
The patient's capabilities are highly above average with anxious depressive symptoms with phobic elements. Psychotic signs cannot be seen. Reality control is adequate.

If anybody still doubts it, here is the proof.

I am brilliant, grim, unsociable, and distrustful. A true catch! For what it's worth, this was in 2008, and I was depressed during the tests. Hopefully, it showed in the results.

I want to conclude by returning to the beginning of this chapter. I'm not a genius. Even if I took another test and it showed my IQ to be 150. A genius proves himself with his actions, not words.

Email to Friends

:):

December 16, 2008

I won't write to you individually because I don't know what I would write to each one of you. That's why I'm writing a single email to explain what's going on and what I think about you and your behavior.

I find it utterly stupid that even after I went to a psychiatrist as you asked me to, I paid 70 euros plus 50 for psychological testing that showed I'm fine, besides being too optimistic and having unrealistic goals and wishes. But the paranoia continues. You demand I get some pills. To calm down and sleep more. How in the hell do you know how much I sleep? Do you want me to stop drinking? Look around you! Look at yourselves!

You disappoint me again and again—you, who were supposed to be my friends. You, whom I chose, let into my inner circle, and trusted with things I told no one else about. You, whom I love and would do anything for. You, who were supposed to be light-bringers, people of the new era, those who will change the world into a nicer place.
You, who call yourselves The Relaxed.

Today I am disappointed. Angry. Sad. Lonely. I may clear my mind in Cuba and put things in their place. Maybe not. Whatever happens, the decision to leave Slovenia is made and final. My first destination after Cuba will be New York. As so many have done before me, I will embark on an adventure of finding myself and new opportunities. It's also an ideal place for artists. I'm optimistic I'll get much inspiration for writing, maybe even drawing. Where to after that? I have no idea, and I like it this way. I've never gazed much into the future. This thing here is an exception.

Don't take this email the wrong way. I love you, and I'm happy to know you. But you've disappointed me in these past few weeks. I'm not mad at you. Just upset. I'm not running away. I'm moving forward.

I love you.

Jaka

Closed Ward

:):

People usually want to know what it's like in a psychiatric institution. Some ask directly, others take detours, and some wait until I start talking about the time I've spent inside. It's not hard for me to talk about it, but my memory is very blurred. I remember some scenes very vividly and others not at all. But it's best to start at the beginning.

I've already described my first contact with Psychiatric Clinic Ljubljana (better known in Slovenia under its nickname Polje, after the city district by that name). Two memories intertwine. In the first one, I was strapped to the bed. In the second, I slept through the first night in my own room. There is a slight chance that both happened. If you make problems, you quickly find yourself tied down. I remember that at first I thought it was a prank. That my friends would run into the room and yell, "Surprise!" The genuine surprise came in the shape of the discovery that my friends weren't coming and that it was a real deal.

When you're strapped down, the animal survival instincts kick in. You yell, roll, and try to get your extremities out of the straps. If you make it, the victorious feelings are very brief and bittersweet. You find out they can tie you in more than one way. If at first you could move your arms so you could eat and drink, that luxury is suddenly gone. If you continue resisting, they tie you across the waist, and you find yourself almost immobilized, waiting for a psychiatrist who comes by six times a day to decide if you're ready to regain your dignity.

I've already mentioned that I was strapped down for eleven days. But that wasn't my worst experience with straps, because most of the time, I wasn't aware of myself or the surroundings. The worst were the days I was (almost) conscious. Time ran really slowly, and because I wasn't stable yet (if I were, I wouldn't have been tied), I tried all kinds of tricks to convince the staff to let me go, at least to go to the toilet. But they've seen and heard it all, so in most cases, your pleas are wishful thinking. So I returned to waiting for a doctor to come by and cursed him when he decided I'd have to wait another four hours.

The straps are undoubtedly an unpleasant experience, but it was probably necessary for the condition I usually arrived in. Every time they unstrapped me, I celebrated on the inside. If nothing else, I began to cherish freedom and the ability to move. When I went to the toilet after a few days (sometimes they untie you, and you can go), I could shower, smoke a cigarette, and call my parents and friends. Things I always took for granted suddenly gained enormous value. Straps are a Therapy with capital *T* and an actual test of oneself. They dehumanize you at some point, but if you don't surrender, it's just like severe depression. You fall apart, take the pieces, and rebuild yourself into a stronger human being.

The closed ward isn't the worst place, but your freedom is limited. For instance, cell phones aren't allowed. You can use old-school phones sticking out of the wall. The phones operate on calling cards that are a valuable asset, even a currency. You can also use, for a very limited time, a computer connected to the Internet. It can become wild around the computer, as patients have to agree on who will be able to dive into the vastness of the World Wide Web and for how long. Because no one is wholly composed, normal conversations are an exception. The most valuable currency in the closed ward is cigarettes, and the smoking room is the place where opinions clash and crazy ideas pop to mind. Because you can't have your lighter, you must light the cigarettes with the lighter in the office, which hangs on a strip. Once a day, a small group of chosen ones goes to a cottage that is basically a small bar and a shop. They don't accept cigarettes or phone cards but sell them for cash. The group collects orders from other patients and delivers the goods.

For me, the best part of the day was visiting hours. I want to thank from the heart everyone who came to see me, mostly my mom and dad, who were there every day, except when I wanted to be alone (which was very rare). Many other brothers- and sisters-in-arms weren't that lucky, and some noticed that my parents immensely loved me. I came to the same conclusion myself, despite quarrels in the past. I will never forget that I wasn't left behind.

Visits can be pretty bizarre. One time, while heavily

sedated with Haldol, I was sitting with a friend, holding my eyes open with my fingers because they wouldn't stay open. Sometimes I could barely speak. I often couldn't sit still, so I paced across the room, left it, and returned. On more than one occasion, I went for a smoke and left the visitors to talk with themselves. "Tomc, don't you have visitors?" was a common question from the staff. Some people think you have no interest in them, but the reality is that "restless feet" are a common side effect of meds, and you can't do anything about it. You want to listen to your visitors. You know they would like to hear your stories. But when the tingling sensation in your legs starts, you get up and go. That's how it is.

Almost every visitor bears gifts. For me, the most desired goods were cigarettes, sweets, soda, snacks, and phone cards. My dad usually also brought me a sandwich that he made himself.
Just like he made them for my mom and me every morning so we could eat them at the office until he was too weak. My mom makes excellent sandwiches, but my dad was a grand master. I regret I never told him that in person, but I'm sure he knew it. That he knows.

Visits, pleasant and not so pleasant, constitute a small portion of the day. But the day passes faster than one would think. Mornings pass quickly. Usually, the day started dragging after lunch. There are no activities, and they don't let you lie in bed because they want your "vacation" to be as active as possible. So what's left is to talk with other patients, which can be strange due to digestion and med effects.

But now and then I hit the jackpot and got into a fruitful, constructive, and utterly exciting conversation. It made me realize I was locked in with open-minded and softhearted thinkers. I'm still in contact with some of them, and glad our paths crossed.

When the visiting hours are over, it's almost time for dinner, followed by evening television watching, which can get feisty as people have to decide what to watch. Surprisingly, there were never any serious arguments. I didn't care what we watched. I didn't have the concentration to follow it anyway.

Another exciting thing happens in the closed ward. A thing that's rarely talked about.
Table tennis tournaments! I don't know what you thought it was going to be, but table tennis matches are so therapeutic that they shorten your stay for a day or two. That is, if you don't get in a fight with your opponent because he argues that the ball touched the table, and you're pretty sure that it didn't. But in most cases, the matches went by calmly and reasonably and brought positive energy. Sometimes a staff member joined us, and I have to admit they were pretty good. Of course, you must let them win if you don't want to lose your privileges.

And so, between waking up, morning exercise, breakfast, morning therapy, therapeutic workshops, lunch, talks, looking for places to lie down, debates in the smoking room, phone conversations, visitations, dinner, table tennis, television, showering, evening therapy, and sleep, life happens in the closed department of Polje hospital. I was there ten times, and even if the experiences weren't the most pleasant of my life, they were undoubtedly the experiences that marked me and prepared me better for life. Even if those weren't the worst of times, I was genuinely excited about the doctors' rounds, especially when it was time to go to the open section.

Manic Promises

:):

February 7, 2009

My dearest. Yesterday evening was quite bizarre, and it continued in an odd morning. So I thought about things this morning while walking from Zupanciceva Jama to Bavarski Dvor, and I came to some conclusions:

1. No more spirits. From now on, only beer and wine. Mostly wine.

2. No more drugs, except pot. No more eating, sniffing, or smoking pills.

3. I will never again ask anybody for coffee, lunch, a party, whatever. If you'd like to see me, call me. If not, I'm okay with it.

4. I will never again bother women who don't have an interest in me. I will delete from my phone the ones who aren't single. Others are potential candidates but have to abide by conclusion 3.

5. I will never again explain what I'm trying to do with my life, where I'm going, and how I'll make my money.

6. Never again will anyone lend or give me money for coffee, pizza, a taxi, an entrance fee, bus fare, drugs, alcohol, bread, condoms, or any other product. All the money I owe will be returned, and that is that.

7. I will never again organize events or form clubs, societies, or groups on Facebook that are meant to change the world for the better. I will no longer pretend that you care about anybody else but yourselves. I will no longer live in a fucking illusion that anyone would like to do anything for others.

One of my friends replied to my email.

1. Maybe remove Article 1.

2. With drugs, I recommend only legal pills. You can get the prescriptions from your doctor.

3. I always like to see you sober and composed.

4. OK.

5. Did you ever consider we are asking you things because we want to help you?
6. Good to hear.

7. Jaka, first you must take care of yourself, then try to change the world, let alone help others. If you can say that WE don't care about anybody else, ask yourself why we didn't leave you sleeping outside yesterday and why the whole evening revolved around you.

JAKA TOMC

Opening Chakras

:):

During a certain period of my life, I was wholeheartedly into spirituality. That wouldn't be anything special, but I was completely indifferent about it before that. I believed in certain things; I just didn't dedicate myself to any of them. In 2005 everything turned around when I entered a meditation group. I quickly changed my perspective on life, the universe, and everything else.

In principle, the group practiced Osho's meditations. In reality, they were combined with kriya, tantra, and more. I started learning Reiki to enhance my spiritual potential even further (I made two levels). For a magazine I wrote for, I came in contact with several world-known spiritual gurus and joined some very intensive workshops. Before I traveled to India for a month, I quit eating meat and persisted for a year. The latter brings back bad memories, not because I missed consuming meat but because I started forcing my new philosophy onto others. When my meatless escapade was inevitably ending, I was so confused about food my vegetarian coworker ordered me to start eating meat again. Not everything is for everyone.

In my book *Manic Poet*, I wrote that meditation is dangerous. I will correct myself this time and say that meditation is not for everyone, especially if that person has a mental illness or a tendency toward one. I'm positive that intensive meditation has triggered the development of my bipolar disorder. I'm not saying it wouldn't have happened in any case. It probably would have. I'm also not holding a grudge or cursing the universe for dealing me a bad hand of cards. I am who I am because of bipolar disorder, and even though I've had moments when I wished things were different, I'm glad they turned out as they did. Meditation opens a person similarly to mania or alcohol, and they bring everything to the surface, good stuff and bad. Let's see what poured out of me the first time I experienced an episode. . . .

It was the final meditation of the two-day workshop. One hour of meditation, let alone two days, can hit you pretty hard. I was a rookie, but because I'm a being who can let go and follow instructions, I went pretty deep. The last meditation of the workshop was the grand finale. We sat in a circle, held hands, and repeated the mantra *om*. It's a basic mantra, but also very powerful if you say it correctly. I must have done something right because I lost consciousness at a particular moment. I didn't fall. Everything just went dark. The sound and the room disappeared, and all that was left was me and the darkness. I have no idea how much time passed, but I felt different when I snapped out of it.
We stood up and formed another circle to say goodbye. I was wondering who those people in the room were. I tried to connect their faces with their names, but I couldn't. We hugged, as we always did, but I felt nothing special. Maybe nothing at all. I felt like an empty shell. Like a body without consciousness. I was by no means well grounded.

But that wasn't the end of a bizarre evening. When we came out, I started looking for my car around the parking lot. It wasn't unusual. I often forget where I parked my car. But that time, I had no clue which car was mine. When I finally found it—probably with the help of my ex-girlfriend— I was in for another surprise. I didn't know how to drive a car! I somehow managed to get the vehicle to a road, where it died, and the engine wouldn't start again. What followed was a cherry on the cake. I tried calling my father but couldn't find his name. He was saved in my cell phone under the name *Padre*. If someone had told me on Saturday morning when we started the workshop that I would be like that on Sunday evening, I'd have said he was losing it. Even today, I have no idea what happened that evening, but based on my experience from the past fifteen years, I'm almost sure I woke up depressed from that meditation. How is it possible? I have no idea. All I know is that I felt practically the same in future depressions.

Relax; the story's not over yet. Before it got better, I lost my senses one more time. I can't position it accurately in time, so it may have occurred before the two-day workshop. That time it didn't hit me during the meditation but after it. The teacher and I were talking. Nothing special, just small talk. She asked me something, and I couldn't answer. My brain had shut down. When we got outside, they stripped me above the waist and massaged me with the snow. It instantly woke me up, and everything was back in order. What followed is very important for understanding the problems bipolar people can have when opening their bodies to certain types of energies. After the incident, our teacher suggested I visit a bioenergy therapist. I listened to her and went. I was there for half an hour and remember only small fractions of our conversation. A soul was supposedly at my parents' apartment, and my aura was infected with a spell. The therapist cleaned it and sold me a wooden pendant I had to name and wear for protection. I did, and I waited for something to happen. It wasn't a long wait.

Do you remember when I said that, in my case, it starts with a smile? That time it did as well. I just had no idea what it was. A few days after my bioenergy therapy, I woke up a new person. If I was an empty shell before the visit, everything inside me was babbling afterward. I remember vividly how I was walking the streets of Ljubljana, experiencing them differently than before. I felt like I was ten feet tall. Like I was levitating. At work—I was working at the National Radio and Television then—I was as relaxed as ever. I had a lot of conversations with my colleagues, even those I never spoke with. Life was suddenly beautiful, colorful, and sensual. I was aware of small details, which made me happy—a perfect turn.

I have no idea when I fell back into grayness, but I do know that our meditation teacher pronounced me enlightened. I didn't bother about it very much. Who knows, maybe enlightenment is similar to mania. Because what happened to me that evening was nothing more than a depression that, after "cleansing," became a mania and slowly died away.

I will say something daring but, in my experience, truthful and essential. Bipolars have to be "dirty" to some extent, may it be from medication, other substances, energy blockages, negative thoughts, or everyday problems. If we "clean" our bodies or psyches too much, there's a severe danger that we'll be catapulted to heights again. Let's see another example that includes energy cleansing.

A few years later, when I'd been diagnosed and was crawling through one of my depressions, a friend recommended another energy healer. I started visiting her every week. We opened chakra after chakra. I felt better after each therapy. Better? I felt great. When that morning smile returned, I was back on track. As with every mania, I thought I could control it that time. That it would never end, and if it did, it would end naturally. Let's be sincere and think logically for a moment. Everything comes to an end. Even the universe and everything that exists will eventually cease to exist. That's how it is and how it is supposed to be. But we don't think about our mortality daily (it seems some people never do), so we don't ponder when mania will end. You let go and ride the wave that days ago seemed like it could be fatal. When you're up, you don't bother with the bottom anymore. When you feel again, you want to feel more. When your brain starts working again, you want to think. You want to understand the structure of life. You want to know it all. You want to experience everything. You are an emotional, thinking being that needs experience. You return to basics, and that's the beauty of mania. As I said, you dare to be you in your purest form. Who would say no to that? If mania was in the form of a pill, it would be a worldwide hit.

I'm sure of that.

Because of the mentioned examples, I believe intense work with energies is inappropriate for bipolar people. Basic meditation, yoga, recreation—absolutely. Shaman workshops, astral travels, dynamic meditations, etc.—no, thanks. Of course, we are all individuals, and what works for one doesn't necessarily work for another. The triggers are different too. Making general theories is hard, so it's best to talk about myself and my experience. Some people will find themselves in my stories. Others will think it's not essential. That's how it is.

I imagine that some readers want to know if I reconnected or remained connected to my spiritual side. Of course I did. I believe every experience is vital for a human being, and we must make the most of it. Even if you drop some activities, there's nothing wrong with it. It's natural. Just like people come and go through time, our actions and worldview change during our lifetime. The saying that people don't change is complete nonsense. We change, all of us. Some of us more, some less. Change is the only constant. It's the irrefutable truth, a law of nature. My connection with spirituality changed through time and still does. At first, I worshipped it, devouring new knowledge. For me, it was something completely new that demolished my view of life and the world and built it anew. This was followed by a period of breakup. At that time, I hated spirituality. I despised everything about it and blamed it for everything that had happened to me. Then came the regeneration period. I was shattered into so many pieces, I needed seven or eight years to put myself back together.

During that period, I was confused. In my apartment, I had a small altar for ten years. Until I moved out, I dared not touch it. I thought something terrible would happen if I did. There's nothing wrong with having an altar at home. A lot of people have places where they keep things they deem holy. But when that altar starts to interfere with your life to a point where you can't make rational decisions anymore, you have a problem. The late Indian guru Sai Baba once said, "The hands that serve are holier than lips that pray." Just like the altar, there's nothing wrong with prayers. I pray from time to time. To no god in particular, but I pray. But when I'm tired after a workout, I feel better than when I pray for feeling well. Every time somebody mentions praying, I remember a joke. There was a man who prayed every day to win a lottery. One day God had had enough of him, and he said, "You will win, but first buy a lottery ticket."

It's been a while since I practiced Reiki. I charged for therapy only once, and even then, my patient got sick. That isn't unusual or bad, but I didn't feel good about it. While writing an article about him, I could still hear a bioenergy therapist saying that I wouldn't be a successful healer because I had too much suppressed negative energy inside me. I did perform a few more therapies on friends or myself. Sometimes I feel that Reiki "turns on," but I don't pay much attention to it. Everything happens for a reason.

After that one-year episode of vegetarianism, I dropped it. I have no issues with it, and I don't try to convince vegans they should eat meat. Maybe I need to eat it because of my blood group (O), or perhaps I just like the taste. I do know that I feel a lot better than I did back then. That's it. When the world switches to a vegan diet, I'll adapt. Until then, I won't complicate my life but eat what I feel like.

There is nothing wrong with spirituality. My problem is letting certain things get to me, and I start losing control. That's why I hope you'll listen to what I say but not take it as instruction. This is not a manual on how to live your life. This is my story. Everybody has one. You can believe in God (or gods), be sure a soul exists, or have blood sausage as your favorite food. Each person is unique. Let's allow ourselves that uniqueness and respect it. Let's respect others and ourselves. Never forget about yourself.

Mania Is Not the End. It's the Beginning.

:):

Mania is lovely until it reaches its final phase, hypermania, and becomes unstable. When you're hypomanic, everything is beautiful, you love everybody, and your energy level is massive and drives you day and night. But when hypermania takes over, your house of cards begins tumbling down. In my case, it always started with delusions, a mixture of reality and imagination. Let's look at a few examples so you get a better feel for it.

My first manic episode dates to a few years before my diagnosis. I was reminded of it by a former coworker and, to this day, a good friend. I'm unsure if my actions resulted from mania, burnout, or a onetime psychosis. But because I know a lot about mania today, I reckon it was the former.

It happened at National Radio and Television, where I was employed then. I believe it was 2005. My last assignment of that evening was preparing news for the night program. I had done my part, said goodbyes, and left. My friend, the editor, as usual, checked the content before his shift ended. When he started reading my articles, he went pale. Instead of news summaries, I'd written my own stories. Most were about our boss, with whom I was on a kind of warpath then. In those short snippets, I wrote everything I thought about him. If my friend hadn't checked them, they would have been broadcast all night. Or at least until someone noticed. He called me in the morning, told me what I'd done, and suggested I make some changes. Seventeen years later, he told me he had been apprehensive about me then and believed that was the start of my bipolar disorder.

During my next mania, which was much more apparent, I realized we were working on something big and vital. At that time, I was working on an EU project. I imagined we were living in two worlds. The first, real one was just a cover for the other one, which ran simultaneously in a parallel dimension and had a higher purpose. Everything I'd seen in my and my coworkers' offices fitted perfectly with my story. I had noticed secret smiles on people I'd spent workdays with, picked up on body language that I usually didn't see, and carefully listened to the words that came out of their mouths. I was piecing together a puzzle, a new truth. I felt like Columbus when he discovered the New World. People around me knew that something odd was happening, especially those I'd called in the evening, asking them if they were coming to Brussels, where the intergalactic meeting was happening.

In the end, I was the one who didn't attend the meeting. Officially because I fell asleep, but in reality, I woke up in the morning and couldn't tell if the meeting was real. I didn't know if it was just in my head or if I should get dressed, drive to the airport, and fly to the European capital. By the time I figured out that the meeting really was happening, it was too late. The looks on my colleagues' faces when I appeared in the office were priceless. So was the director's sermon. Here's how my former coworker described that day:

That was the day when you were supposed to go to Brussels again. The director told me to check on you to see if you'd actually gone. (We were beginning to suspect something was happening.) When you finally answered my phone call, you told me you hadn't gone. All hell broke loose, as the tickets and the hotel room were paid for.

But you said, "You know what? I figured out that the meeting was happening in any case. So I didn't go. And love will win." Later you came to the office in a sari [it wasn't a sari but a lungi, a sort of men's skirt], delighted. The director started losing it, but you joyfully repeated the mantra that love would win.

Of course, I received a special award—a meeting with a psychiatrist. It went very well. I stuck to the story that I had overslept because I'd argued with my girlfriend all night, and didn't go into details (a huge success when you're manic). I answered the questions shortly and concisely. Epilogue? The record went into my file, and I received a warning. Case closed.

My next mania, which I've already written about, occurred in 2007, before my first hospitalization. It lasted a record length of time, from spring until the end of the year.

The people closest to me noticed that something was odd. My friend wrote an article about my fight with the disease.

We noticed that Jaka wasn't our Jaka anymore. At first, we thought he wanted to enjoy life fully after a breakup with his girlfriend. He was so excited. All the time. He was online and on Facebook day and night. He had his phone in his hands all the time. He didn't miss a single party. His nights out turned into days. His tempo was impossible to follow.

When I look at that time today, from a distance and with a sober mind, parties were one thing that held me together because they made me use a lot of surplus energy. But when the planets aligned in one moment, the boiling water the lid had held in place for months overflowed.

Let's fast-forward a few years. I was pretty manic when I went jogging around Ljubljana. Physical activity should help with mania, but on that occasion the condition worsened instead. During the run, I realized I was superhuman. A genetically modified subject, born, raised, and trained for higher goals. What were those goals? I never found out. I did find other superhumans nearby, but they weren't aware of their pedigree, so they looked confused when I spoke to them and opened that subject.

Let's return to my running endeavor. After three hundred meters, I took off my T-shirt. I was fitter then than during the writing of this book, so the whole picture was easier to digest. Nevertheless, it wasn't my normal behavior.

When I reached Wolfova Street, I started calling for the mayor. "Zo-ran! ZO-RAN!" I can shout very loudly, and incredibly loudly when I'm manic, so it was probably quite scary for the bystanders. I reached Zvezda café, where I walked up to a random guy sitting with a woman at one of the outdoor tables.

"Give me the tie," I said to him calmly.

He just stared at me. "What?"

"The tie. Please give it to me. I'm going to see the mayor."

"What?"

I grabbed his tie and started pulling. Somebody must have stopped me. Maybe I stopped myself. In any case, nobody got hurt. So I went to City Hall as I was, in sweatpants, without a T-shirt, and wearing a grim look on my face. I ran to the building, went to the press conference room on the first floor, switched on the microphone, and said, "BOO." That was it. I ran down the stairs past the security guard and continued to the old town. During the jog, I got a fascinating idea that I could run through people. Luckily I wasn't losing it completely, and I theatrically turned before hitting anybody except for one fellow. If I had plowed through him with my hundred-plus kilograms, full sprint, it could have ended tragically. I think I did hurt his hand, though. The one that met my face. I just bounced away and ran—to the studio of Vest, where I crashed on the couch.

I think the police were looking for me, but my coworkers talked them out of it. I could rest myself and postpone another trip to the hospital, if only for a few days.

In one of my next hypermanias, I pretended I was a time traveler. Yes, you've read it correctly. I pretended. At first, I was fully aware the thing was a joke, a show, a performance. A few hours later, I was convinced it was for real, and I fully accepted the role of a person who can travel through time and space. What did my spectacle look like? In my most impressive scenes, I ran, jumped, and landed in front of unsuspecting people and asked them what year it was. Or what planet I was on. I must admit I was having a lot of fun when I was still in control. I don't know what the people who became part of my show were thinking, but I couldn't care less. Soon I upgraded my gig. The most efficient way of surprising people was when I walked behind them, then loudly said "whoosh," so they turned around shocked. I put my poker face on and looked around, trying to figure out where and when I was. Wild, I tell you.

The stories I'm telling you are, to some extent, fun. The ones where I completely lost it, not so much. Those are the ones I regret the most because people who didn't deserve it were hurt. I'm talking about a friend who listened to me shouting "She's a whore!" in front of her house. An acquaintance I pinned to the wall at Daktari, where we occasionally hung out, because I thought he'd stolen my cell phone. My father, whom I tried to choke because he grabbed my hand while I was pouring the contents of his whiskey bottle into the sink.

I couldn't help myself at those moments, but that was no excuse.

I'm not an aggressive person, even when drunk. Nevertheless, I grabbed a road sign once and threw it amongst people at the open market while shouting I was the last Jew in Ljubljana. I'm not Jewish, and I threw the sign in an area that wasn't full of people, but I scared some of them. The police intercepted me at Prešeren Square minutes later, by which time I'd forgotten what I'd done. Luckily a tourist came by, told the police the whole story, and put the finger on me so there would be no doubt who the culprit was. The prize came in the form of a yellow and orange ambulance van that generously drove me to the all-inclusive resort. When you've been inside a few times, you get used to the fact that the end of the story is always the same. Even if I desired immensely that they'd let me finish the cycle and fall back down alone. You see, mania is the same as depression but reversed. When you're on top, the only way is down.

The way down is much more challenging and painful than the way up. It's logical, and you expect it, but you're still shocked. With me, the falling started when I was still a free man. All of the above stories happened at the end of manic cycles. But unfortunately (or luckily), I never walked those final steps to the edge alone. My fellow passengers were antipsychotics, stabilizers, and tranquilizers. When the road became really steep, the antidepressant joined our fellowship. The time in the hospital is precious, and there's always a shortage of empty beds. That means no one will wait for you to fall naturally, whether you're a veteran or not.

Have I mentioned the day when I thought I was the resistance leader in *The Terminator*? How about that one when I was sure I was a dragon? Or the one when I was scared the Satanists would sacrifice my ex-girlfriend? Well, I most certainly haven't told you about a bizarre evening when I took a Seroquel because somebody (not me) thought it was a good idea and would make me sleep. I was lying in bed, waiting for the medicine to hit me, when I suddenly noticed that somebody or something was harvesting my inseminated eggs. Hold on. Is that a typo? It is not. I was lying in bed, thinking I was the queen mother of some alien race, waiting for them to harvest my embryos and let me be. That evening ended at the police station, where I insisted on going. I had no chance there. I probably babbled about bipolar disorder, preaching how wonderful it was. While I was smoking outside, I was explaining to a police officer that I was a then-famous Higgs boson and thus presented a terrible danger to our city and the world. There are no winners after a debate like that, only losers.

The Terminator. I don't recall how that day began, nor can I put a time stamp on it. I believe it happened on the same day I walked to the castle. What's so special about that? I climbed the castle hill. I went straight up, barefooted. I left my shoes with a group of German tourists chilling at one of the benches along the path, drinking beer. Then I went up, through the bushes and rocks, across the glass shards and fences, to my destination. When I arrived at the top, I spread my wings and waved to other hikers. Wings? Have I not mentioned that I was sure I was an angel? When I came back down, I walked to a café called Cacao. I was sitting there, dirty, barefoot, in an original Slovene Army T-shirt. One of the servers probably noticed something odd going on with me, so he brought me free ice cream. Maybe he thought I was a war veteran. He was perhaps friendly and understanding and noticed I needed something for my stomach and soul. Suddenly a woman and her daughter sat down opposite me. We talked a bit, they ordered their drinks, and then the paranoia hit me. I thought the little one could read my mind. If they had sent such a skillful person to get me, I had to be somebody important. I said goodbye and walked toward Maček.

During the walk, I concluded that we were at war with the machines, and I was one of the remaining hopes for humanity. As their leader, a Slovene John Connor, I had to do something about it. So I started recruiting human soldiers for the imminent battle. As usual, the puzzle pieces fell into place and coincided with my delusions. When I sat at the table outside the pub, I noticed a soldier sitting at one of the other tables. It's possible he was a soldier solely in my head, but he had a genuine military rucksack. Something bothered me, so I grabbed his backpack and threw it on the street. "You're not coming with us!" I yelled at him and walked away. People were utterly ignorant of the threat the killing robots presented for our planet, and I was sad because, again, I had to deal with it alone.

While you're likable to most people when hypomanic, and they usually gladly invite you into their circle (even if you sometimes kind of force it), they start avoiding you when you're hypermanic. I had to listen to stuff like

"Fuck, Tomc is coming. There's going to be trouble again." Sometimes I barely avoided physical confrontation. I met a guy at a gas station and invited him and his friend to my place. While his friend slept on my couch, the guy and I went to Metelkova (an autonomous cultural zone in Ljubljana). He was wrapped in the Slovene flag, shouting that his name was Dolfe (a version of Adolf), and I was guarding him with a broom, pretending it was a sniper rifle.

That was not the first time I thought I was a sniper. Once, I walked around the city with my SLR camera, which I already mentioned. I didn't care much about photography before I went to Poreč, Croatia, met a Russian photographer, and tested her camera. The photos were fantastic, and I decided I desperately needed that apparatus in my life, even if it cost me a thousand euros. We've taken countless pictures at numerous parties and events and met many people that way. A few years later, I used the camera for my shooting spree across Ljubljana. I knew the camera was not a weapon. I was training for the times when shit would hit the fan. I soon put together a story that my father and I were elite special forces members. He was a retired officer and member of an anti-aircraft unit, and I was a talented sniper. Maybe you're asking yourself who was supposed to attack us. I have no idea. Perhaps the answer lies in the episode where I was a member of the intergalactic police. Unfortunately, that's all I can tell you about that episode because they erased my memory.

The following story started with me throwing objects out the window and ended like a Hollywood movie.

I don't know what made me so mad. Maybe I wasn't even angry; it was one of my cleaning sprees where I tried to remove stuff that was burdening me. Sometimes it was negative energy; sometimes it was things that reminded me of certain people; and sometimes it was just a moment of insanity. That time it was pretty dangerous, as I was throwing things on the sidewalk next to the building. I think I checked before I threw each item, but that doesn't change the fact that my doing that could have hurt someone. Somebody called the cops. If I remember correctly, they were already there when I came down. I might have been topless, or perhaps I took my shirt off in front of the police. I do know that I marched to the Poljane secondary school, knelt down, and put my hands on the back of my head. Police car lights were blinking around me. Some of you will remember the scene from the movie *American History X* where Derek Vinyard (played by Edward Norton) kneels when the cops arrest him. I've re-created that scene in real life, and it wasn't a coincidence. I wanted to do it. I knew what was coming and wanted to go in style, like a man. And down I went, off to another vacation at the psychiatric clinic.

That wasn't the only time my things were flying out the window. A few years later, it started with my laptop. I threw it off the balcony to the park below. Then I also threw some other stuff out, including expensive photographs hanging on the walls. Sometimes during those moments of temporary insanity, I wondered if I could jump out myself. I'm positive that it could've happened. Some people say the balcony is calling them. My balcony, luckily, liked nonliving things more.

JAKA TOMC

It's crystal clear now that I like to remove the upper pieces of clothing when I'm manic. Let's talk about shouting for a moment—loud shouting. Maybe you're pondering whether shouting can be anything other than loud. It can. I'm talking about extreme shouting, the loudest your body allows. Calling the mayor's name was just a warm-up—an exercise for what would come in one of my next manias.

The memories of that event are blurry and split into dozens of pieces. That's why I'll probably group several days into one. One morning the hypermanic me walked into the city center. Not far from my apartment, an older guy was maneuvering his vehicle. Maybe he started maneuvering because he saw me approaching. I might have started shouting at him, because he almost hit me with his car and, in that short moment of sheer terror, pressed the gas pedal and clutch simultaneously and tried to drive away. I don't know the exact words I used, but I know he was petrified. I would have been too.

I walked on, did a tour of Trubarjeva Street, and didn't have to wait long for something to happen. A guy on his moped was driving toward me. I could have stepped out of his way, but of course I didn't. I grabbed the handlebar, stopping the moped immediately. "Pedestrian zone," I said calmly. He just looked at me, confused. It was 7 a.m., and he was probably on his way to work. He surely didn't expect a hand brake in the shape of a grown man. There were no complications, so we each went our own way. I accepted my role as a city policeman, caring for people in the pedestrian zones. Even when I'm not manic, I don't like cyclists or people on scooters, mopeds, and other means of transport in zones meant for people moving on feet. But I won't argue about the city policies. Let's get back to the story.

I was standing on the Breg when I spotted a cyclist closing in on me. It was a beautiful morning, so she was gazing at nature, people, bars, and shops. Not the slightest worry was on her mind. Of course, she didn't expect somebody not to move out of her way. I had other plans. I stood my ground and turned sideways. She hit me at cruising speed and fell. She was looking at me, shocked, and said, "You hit me." I responded, "No, you hit me." It was her word against mine. She was a respected senior citizen.
I was too manic for a decent defense. The real municipal police came. Order was restored, and I received a ticket. Better than a ticket to the hospital, I thought. But the latter was inevitable. It always is.

JAKA TOMC

Letter to Friends

:):

Ljubljana, January 31, 2013

I've been pondering the thought of telling you how I feel for quite a while now, but I've been putting it off because what's the point? People have enough of their own problems. They don't need mine as well. But I need to get this out of me because it aches and burdens me. As I don't put two connected sentences together at live meetings, I've decided I'll write this letter slowly and try to capture the momentary state of my soul.

I'm so tired. Tired of all the thinking. Tired of analyzing myself. Tired of figuring out why things are what they are. I'm ashamed. Ashamed of the things I've done during my manic episodes. I'm sorry for the people I've hurt. People who stood by me and tried to help me, but I didn't listen. I'm ashamed of the words I've said, even if I don't remember most of them. Many are written in my everyday chats and text messages that I bothered people with. When I started reading them, everything went black before my eyes because I realized what a fool I was. That was when the last brick fell off my wall of the idea that I'm relaxed, cool, and likable when manic. Actually, I'm demanding, selfish, and rude.

I talk a lot, which is fine, but most of it doesn't make sense.

I've decided that I don't want another manic phase. Ever. I've made a fool of myself too many times. I've sought copious amounts of attention at every step. I've tried to show the world I'm here. Yes, it felt good, but I was alone in this distorted image of reality.

It's so easy to say, "What has been done has been done. Let's move on." Every day I talk with myself about baby steps and small victories, and when I think things are improving, some invisible force stops me and throws me back on my ass. One step forward, two steps back. But what if that step forward is barely visible, and backward is a fair leap? It was worse, much worse than it is now. There was a time I was lying on a sofa, shaking, because I was sure someone would come and do something to me. I didn't dare to leave the flat. I couldn't be still. I had to move as soon as I sat down or lay down. Once I got myself together a little, I had to deal with the outside world. I know that friends want to help you when they lure you out, for some fresh air, for a walk, for a coffee, but those who haven't been there themselves cannot know how stressful and tiring it can be to sit in a pub or walk around the city. When you think everyone is looking at you, judging you, knowing something is wrong with you. I've had severe panic attacks several times when I could not move. It can be quite distressing if you're on a bus and there's a station coming up where you're supposed to get off.

I'm not talking much at the moment. Most of the time, I answer questions or agree with something someone has said. That's why I'm uncomfortable meeting people or calling them. But I want to. I often feel like picking up the phone and calling someone. Sometimes I do. But then, after a few—usually pre-prepared—sentences, I run out of steam and wait for the conversation to end as soon as possible. It's the same with meeting people over coffee. The good thing is that I meet people with a lot to say because leading the conversation myself would be devastating.

It's a fact that after those coffees, I feel worse than before. It seems everybody has a lot of ideas, desires, dreams, goals, and opinions; I feel completely worthless. I'm also slow at grasping things. While I'm pondering one issue, the conversation usually continues, and I often miss my chance to reply. Conversations with several people at once are the most difficult. They are challenging to follow, and I try to avoid them. My memory is seriously fucking with me, and I'm scared it's a permanent malfunction. And since the conversation over coffee often turns to "Do you remember?," these are really stressful moments for me. Usually, I remember only fragments or nothing at all, and when it comes to who said what, my mind completely shuts down. If somebody recites a conversation from a couple of years ago, it's not very encouraging; no hard feelings. I feel bad about all the good debates, wise advice, and beautiful moments probably lost forever. Maybe some of you think this is not such a big problem. For me, it's enormous.

I'm not writing anymore, and I don't believe I'll ever publish another book. I guess the people who said my writing is just another pose were right. I'm not satisfied with the books I've published, and at this moment, I don't feel even remotely capable of writing anything better. I'm sorry for Manic Poet, *which could have been a brilliant book that would've actually helped people with bipolar disorder and their loved ones. Instead, I feel it's just a confused collection of words with no deeper meaning.*

I find everyday tasks, which are routine for most, burdensome. Buying groceries at the store, for example. At least now I don't have that problem of panicking about people in the store. But it is incredibly annoying to go into a store and stare at the shelves to figure out what I should buy. While I look around, everybody else throws stuff in their baskets and trolleys, knowing precisely what they'll eat for lunch or dinner, and then even buys food for the next day's breakfast. Meanwhile, I am staring at the yogurts, wondering if I should buy one. So people say to me, "Make a list." Fair enough. If I hadn't spent half an hour looking at a blank piece of paper, pondering what to write. Not to mention buying clothes, which I avoid, even though I have one pair of jeans, two old cardigans, and a couple of sweaters I dislike. It makes the mornings very stressful when it comes to getting dressed. At work, I always tactfully go to lunch at a time when I know no one will be there, so I don't accidentally talk to anyone. And all this is killing me—day after day.

Besides what I mentioned, people ask me if I have a girlfriend. My dear friends, tell me, what can I give to a woman? I'm sure everyone's dreams are to get into her life a quiet, depressed, shy man who can barely care for himself. A man who doesn't believe in himself. A man who doesn't know if he can function in this world. How can I love someone if I don't love myself? "Try and find out" is not good advice, and it seems utterly pointless to me, even if it's well-intentioned. It's better I miss a chance than get burned and crushed.

This is just a part of the thoughts running through my mind, but I spent more than two hours putting it into words, and I think it's enough. Thank you for being by my side, some of you actually, others in your thoughts. I know you want me to be well; I just wanted to explain how I experience some of these things. I promise to keep fighting, and I believe you will help me win this battle. I love you.

Jaka

JAKA TOMC

How to Prepare Yourself?

:):

I used to think that I couldn't prepare for depression and mania. That they could completely surprise me and sneak through the window while I was guarding the front door. Fifteen years later, I know that even if they can still surprise me, I've learned to observe my body and feelings to the point where I can detect quite well if I'm moving up or down on the mood scale.

I've already mentioned butterflies in the stomach and vibrating during hypomania. The main problem isn't that you can't feel or recognize it when it comes. I am talking about those of us who aren't experiencing it for the first time. The critical decision is whether you open the door when it comes knocking. Of course, it's not that simple. A closed door doesn't mean it will just waltz away. But it's the first and the most crucial step you can make, and an extremely difficult one—especially if you're recovering after depression or your life isn't what you want it to be. When you're weak, vulnerable, and unhappy, when you need a breath of fresh air, a new lease on life, or a lifeline, you won't be standing behind closed doors for long.

JAKA TOMC

Would you give up the sudden arrival of fresh, warm, and colorful energy after a few years of wandering in the grayness of mediocrity? Would you confide in someone and tell them you feel better and that it's not good for you? Would you accept that a shift in your mood from a four to a seven on a scale of ten is a sign of alarm? I didn't for many years. I thought I could peek through the ajar door, just enough to freshen up. But it never ended there. I always went all the way, and the ending was the same every time. Until I realized I was running in circles and until I decided to kill my thirst for mania, I was a victim of the disease I'm sharing my body with. That doesn't mean I'm cured. It's not even close. I need to be constantly alert because both mania and depression can exploit a moment of inattention. Sometimes I say I'm always walking on the edge, even if that became an automatism after a few relatively calm years. Nevertheless, I have to stop occasionally and check where I am. Because I don't want to jump up, even though I'm sometimes tempted, and I don't want to fall into the abyss, even though it would sometimes be the easiest thing to do.

When I start falling, I lie down a lot, not so much because I'm tired, even if I am—tired of life. Basically, it's about hiding from the real problems that are waiting for me out there. When a lot of issues that need to be at least addressed, if not solved, pile up, the ground beneath my feet disappears. If I curl up in the fetal position on the sofa or in bed, they disappear, at least for a while. The longer I lie down, the more distant they become. And when they are almost gone, they hit me in the face simultaneously.

At that moment, I have two options. I can get up and tackle one of the problems, or bury my head in the pillow and try to fall asleep. Lying down when depressed is more of a defense mechanism than a sign of fatigue, although as you sink deeper and deeper, you also become more and more physically exhausted.

Another thing I recognize as a sign of impending depression is the desire for solitude and silence. As I'm not overly sociable, it's not easy to spot this either. But still, declining invitations to certain meetings or coffee is a sign that all is not well. There was a period in my life when I would shake if somebody sat next to me during lunch break and wanted to talk. When my friends invited me for drinks because they wanted me to socialize, I didn't answer the phone. I've canceled birthday parties. Ultimately, the most persistent friends invited me for a walk or a drink in silence. These moments were a turning point as I realized something needed to change. Like addressing the problems. Even if the problem is meeting a good friend who's prepared to sit with you in silence so you don't have to walk the whole way out of depression alone.

In depression, your body is incredibly heavy. Every movement demands an extraordinary amount of energy. Maybe it's intentional, so you lie down and preserve your strength. I don't know. I'm guessing. What I do know is that I spent a lot of my energy reliving memories and thinking about my life being the way it is. Of course, my memories and my life's outline at that time were distorted because my position was very negative. If the brain of an average person consumes around 20 percent of the total energy the body needs, my depressed brain used at least 90 percent. At least, that's how it felt.

The worst symptom of depression, at least for me, is numbness. Many times in conversations with people and interviews for the media, I've expressed that sadness was not the problem. When I could cry, the worst was behind me (or it hadn't yet begun). What I fear the most are emptiness, helplessness, and the feeling that you exist and don't exist simultaneously. Sometimes medication also contributes to numbness, and I may have been numb every time I've taken a particular pill or combination of drugs. That doesn't necessarily mean that it's a bad thing. For many, numbness is better than intense sadness, severe pain, or fear. Perhaps it was for me too. But it was also killing me.

I've listed four things that were typical of my depression. The key questions I wanted to address in this chapter are, can we feel depression before it starts its march, and can we stop it? My answer to both questions is yes. From what I've experienced, I believe we can. But here's a bonus question I've already mentioned when I was talking about mania. That question is, *do we want* to stop depression? It may sound silly. Hypomania is beautiful, and our addiction to it is logical. But who would like to be depressed? Let's see.

We can feel depression before it transforms into a devastating hurricane. That's a fact. The more episodes a person endures, the easier it is to feel one coming. How? By paying attention to their well-being, physical and mental.

By paying attention to changes in everyday behavior. To their reactions to events. In short, it is essential to observe oneself. For me, as I mentioned above, there are four symptoms: lounging, a desire for solitude, a heavy and tired body, and numbness. When any of those four signs appear, my alarm goes off. My decision at that time is seemingly simple, as it is reduced to two options: YES or NO. Do I want depression or not? I know I'm being quite presumptuous with this statement, and many people will disagree with me, but that's how it is with me, and I believe I'm not the only one. But why would anyone choose depression if there's nothing good about it? Let me answer with a question. Why would anyone commit suicide? Life and death are at stake. Why would anyone choose death? I leave the answers to you.

I've said that the decision to be depressed is seemingly straightforward, but in reality, it requires a tremendous amount of reflection, usually over a short period of time. We don't have the privilege to say to depression, "Give me a week to think about it, then we'll see." Hesitation is like inviting depression in, saying that it's welcome. People in different life situations need different things to decide what to do, so I can't give you a magical recipe. What I can do is tell you what helps me.

A quick analysis of what the decision would entail is the number one priority. What are the positive and negative consequences? Positive? How can depression be positive? When you're depressed, your life kind of stops. You close yourself off from external problems, which, of course, don't disappear, but eventually become very distant. Lying down and sleeping a lot gives you rest (at least physically). You have a lot of time to get to know yourself. This can also be negative because rummaging through oneself tends to bring up repressed memories, thoughts, and feelings. But there are positive sides to depression, even though it's generally distressing, painful, and, in most cases, long-lasting.

Another thing that helps me decide whether I want to be depressed or not is talking. I'm not a person who talks a lot about his problems—most of the time because I don't want to burden those close to me with additional worries. Which is pretty dumb, because I want my loved ones to entrust their problems to me. Fortunately, I have a therapist whom I can tell practically everything that's bothering me. Win-win.

If I still can't decide after the first two steps, the situation is serious. In that case, I'm in a position where depression is an acceptable choice. This brings us to the question that most people are interested in, whether they are struggling with depression or have family members, friends, or acquaintances who are coping with depression: is it possible to stop depression at this point?

The simple answer is—of course. It's this position on the chessboard when all parameters show we'll be checkmated, but there is still a chance for a draw, which is of the utmost importance. On the one hand, we cannot decide to continue with the rhythm of life as it is at that moment, and on the other hand, we have not yet succumbed to the tentacles of depression.

The situation is highly fragile and depends on our next moves.

My first move is always to list the issues or problems at hand and decide to tackle one of them. But beware! I never do the most challenging thing, even though it would be the first choice for many people because manuals and life coaches teach us to tackle the most complicated puzzle first, the one that weighs us down the most. I can tell you firsthand that when you are staring into the abyss—let alone when you are in it—tackling complex problems is not the best solution. Depression is not Gardaland! When we went there once, my friends convinced me to ride the Blue Tornado first, followed by the free fall. Their tactic was simple. They wanted me to try the most challenging, most adrenaline-pumping rides first. I have to admit their plan was successful. But when you're battling depression, you don't play the hero. It's as if you're skiing downhill on plastic skis. The only tactic that works is to address a solvable problem in the state you're in at the time. It can be pretty trivial. It's even better that it's insignificant. Maybe you need to take out the garbage. Or clean out the closet. Throw away some moldy food from the fridge, perhaps. Check a hundred emails that have piled up in your inbox. My point is that the ladder of problems needs to be tackled from the bottom up and, above all, slowly. Once one task is done, we can tackle another or reward ourselves for doing the first one well. Yes, let's reward ourselves. Try it. You'll see that it feels better than hundreds of likes on social networks.

JAKA TOMC

Anger and Disappointment

:):

Anger is a perfectly natural emotion. So let's clarify that it's okay to be angry sometimes. It's not okay if anger escalates into verbal or physical violence against others or yourself.

I don't recall a mania in which I wasn't mad at someone. Every time somebody or something pissed me off, it just went downhill (actually uphill, but you know what I mean). My reactions to anger varied. Sometimes I screamed; sometimes I cried; sometimes I pinned someone against a wall. I don't remember ever physically hurting anyone. But I've certainly left wounds on a few hearts of people close to me.

I am sure I have a lot of pent-up anger. It may have built up in me for one reason or another; it may have been inherited from my ancestors. It doesn't matter—it is mine now. All I can do is let it out slowly and try not to hurt anyone else.

When manic, you're primarily angry with others, but in depression, you're mad at yourself. This is a very simplistic statement, but in my case, it is true. In my manic periods, I was angry with my parents, partner, friends, bosses, colleagues, medical staff, fellow patients, and even strangers I met on the street. At the time, it seemed perfectly justified, but later I regretted my words and actions. The reasons for my anger varied. Usually, it was enough that someone said something. Or did something. Or didn't do it in a way I thought was right.

In depression, the situation is the opposite. During those phases, I've regretted all the unpleasant events of previous manias. And not just the manias; I've regretted practically everything I had done up to that point. The regret eventually turned into anger. Sometimes I even slapped myself. I was angry because I was the way I was. After all, certain things had or had not happened because of me and because I was pushing people I loved away from me. One of the common fears is fear that we will become like our parents. For me, this fear often turned into anger. When depressed, I was angry at myself for not knowing how to be different; when manic, I was mad at my parents for making me that way.

It's important to remember one thing. Anger is always the consequence, not the cause. That's why we must start to look for and remedy the causes of our anger.

I was mad at my dad for a long time. The reasons were clear. He drank excessively and was often negative, and when he was about fifty, he stopped working. Who wouldn't be angry at him? Who wouldn't be scared to become just like him? I was.

If I think about it, that was responsible for my anger. Whenever I'm pessimistic, I get scared that I am turning into my father. I think of him whenever I reflect on what's happening in the world. I hear his voice whenever I think about today's turbo-capitalism and how it's not my cup of tea. I was angry with my father for holding up a mirror for me. He still does to this day, even though he's no longer with us.

Let's allow ourselves to be angry but work on discovering where this anger comes from. Sometimes we can do it ourselves; sometimes we need a trained person—not to find the causes for us but to help us find the answers for ourselves.

Expressing anger is often a valve. We need to let out the pent-up energy. I suggest sport. One that makes you as tired as possible. If you have to punch, choose boxing or some other martial art. If you have to run, run or play an hour of basketball or football. If you need to howl, go to a game of your favorite club. Or a concert. At home, you can bellow in the bathtub or the sink. Of course, remember to fill them with water first.

Disappointment is also a normal emotion, and nothing is wrong with it. Everyone has been disappointed at least a few times in their life, either because of their own actions (or because of something they did not do) or because of others' activities or lack of them.

When I was manic, I was disappointed mainly by

other people's actions. Usually, they were people close to me, but sometimes they were strangers. When I was hospitalized for the first time, I was highly disappointed. I felt betrayed. I thought we could have solved my problems differently. Whenever my family or friends persuaded me that something was wrong with my behavior, I was disappointed. I thought I knew best what was good for me and could help myself. Almost every time, they turned out to be correct. But during their interventions, I was disappointed because I felt misunderstood. With every disappointment, you start to cut ties you may have built up over years or decades. You cut and cut until you're entirely alone. So you look for new people, strangers. People who won't disappoint you but also won't give you what you need most—love and closeness. You get caught in a spiral of emotions from which you can hardly escape unscathed. In my case, it was always a defining moment that ended in the hospital. I was angry, frustrated, and lonely until the first visitor showed up.

Depression is mainly about being disappointed in yourself. You feel weak, ugly, stupid, and misunderstood. Each time I slid into depression, I was disappointed because I had allowed myself to get caught in the familiar cycle again—mania, hospitalization, depression. Disappointed in the words I had spoken, in the actions I had taken, in the sick mind that had led me into a situation in which I was helpless. Disappointment with oneself usually leads to regret and apology. I'm a person who finds it difficult to apologize to someone's face; I find it easier to do so with the written word.

In any case, it's proper to apologize to the people we've hurt. If you can't do it depressed, wait until the situation improves sufficiently that you can. With every apology, the burden on your shoulders will lighten. Try it and see for yourself.

JAKA TOMC

I'm Sorry for Everything

:):

December 23, 2013

I've been reading old chats, and again, just like every time in this phase, I've found out what an asshole I am when I'm manic. I'm tired of everything, I've lost myself, and I'm petrified that I won't be able to find myself anymore. I'm visiting a therapist now. It's cool, it helps, but the holidays are pulling me down a bit into depression. I expected it, but I thought I'd managed to avoid it because, up until last week, it was pretty alright.

I don't want to lose myself too much in my mind flow. I'm sorry for my scenes in the spring. I'm sorry for yelling at you when you only wished me well. I'm sorry for the public insults. The easiest thing to say would be that I just wasn't myself, that the manic me is some foreign entity inside me, but I'm afraid things aren't that simple. All of it is me, and that's the hardest thing to accept because I'm not like that in a normal phase, let alone the depressed one.

Do you know what the most fucked-up thing is? I'm a junkie. I'm addicted to fucking mania. I can consciously say I don't want it anymore, and I know something terrible will happen, but part of me needs it. The only feasible solution is to prevent it for a few years so that it will be just a fleeting, irrelevant memory. But just like every disease, this one, too, wants to live. It adapts to conditions and medications. I'm scared of plunging into depression, only to jump up again and make trouble for myself and others.

I'm sorry.

Jaka

* * *

During every mania, I've hurt, insulted, or shocked someone. Every time I fell back to the ground, I was sorry. In the previous chapter, I mentioned that I don't like apologizing in person. My grandma said that when I was a little boy, I wrote a letter of apology to my grandpa when I made him sad. That little Jaka is still a part of me, writing letters and emails and apologies through messages or online chats. Why? Because it's easier. Because I capture everything I want to say. Because I can think before I react. Because it's hard to look people in the eyes. I'm not the only one, and an apology is as sincere if you write it as it is if you say it. At least it should be.

I couldn't apologize to some people; they were just extras in my blockbuster movie, and I never saw them again. And I didn't tug at the sleeve of those I did see but didn't know and bother them with apologies. You can never apologize to everyone.

At this point, someone might ask which event I regret the most. It's a good question, but I can't give a simple answer. Some scenes keep running through my mind. Rarely a day goes by when I don't recall an event from one of my manic or depressive phases. Of course, scenes from *normal* times are also spinning in front of my eyes, but because my brain has a life of its own, I quickly find myself in an interesting manic story from the past. I would hardly say that I regret a single event the most. There are many, but because one thing leads to another and I believe that everything happens for a reason, sometimes the consequences of my actions, even if incomprehensible and even dangerous at the time, have been good in the end.

I'm sorry about the people who got screwed because of me. I've clarified my differences with some of them and we're still friends today, while I have parted ways with others. But this is life. People come and go. The most important thing is to be able to live with yourself. So the next time you feel sorry for yourself, remember to apologize and forgive yourself.

JAKA TOMC

Open Ward

:):

In the open ward of a psychiatric hospital (at least in Ljubljana), the situation is—as the name suggests—a lot different than in the closed ward. There are many open wards. I have no idea how they organize who goes where, but what's important to you at that moment is that you're entering a period of greater freedom. If you have your fellows with you with whom you get on well, your future is bright, and your recovery is in sight.

Open ward doesn't provide absolute freedom, although, as far as I know, you can leave whenever you want. Of course, interrupting treatment is not advisable. I've tried it myself. But as it was my first hospitalization and I didn't yet know the "rules of the game," I am forgiven.

In my *career*, I've been in different wards. They aren't only distinguished by their letter-and-number names (I-5, for example) and their appearance, depending on the building they're in. But what matters most to us patients is who is in charge of each ward, i.e., which psychiatrist is in charge of you and your team. Approaches can be very different, and consequently, so can the treatment.

A day in the open ward goes like this: wake up,

exercise, morning therapy (medication), breakfast, rounds, workshops, lunch, rest, afternoon therapy, snack, focus group, dinner, free time, evening therapy, bedtime. Everyone is left to their own devices between activities, meaning you can do practically whatever you want. You shouldn't leave the hospital grounds, but no one will bother you if you walk along the nearby Path of Memories and Comradeship. However, it's best to inform the staff of your intended location. As for free time between activities, that's great at first sight. But once you've been inside for weeks or months and you get tired of the coffee and cakes (they're a sought-after commodity) in the log cabin, a bar (no alcohol) and a store on hospital grounds, your days start to drag. That's when visits come in handy, and unlike in the closed ward, where there's a set time for visits, they can arrive at any time. Visits break the monotony and bring fresh air into your daily life. They also remind you that you're not alone. Some people care about you, love you, and want you to come home as soon as possible.

In an open ward, you usually return home. If you're okay, they'll let you out for the weekend. It can last one day but can also be from Thursday to Sunday. So half the week in the hospital and half at home or wherever. The important thing is that you turn up at your ward on Sunday evening. Some people don't. Weekend outings are generally great, but I've had mixed experiences. You have to be aware that I was taking large amounts of medication. That's why I was never quite present. It was pleasant at home. It wasn't so nice if I was showering and it felt like someone was watching me. Or I was sitting in a popular bar, and my hands were shaking so much that I had to hold the coffee cup with both hands. But most of the time, the time away went by too quickly, and it was painful to go back inside on a Sunday night.

But weekend getaways aren't the only option. The last time I needed treatment, I was in what is known as *daily therapy*. This means I came to the hospital every morning and went home after lunch. Of course, I was also entitled to weekend outings according to the principle described above. The daily therapy regime suited me well, even though I realized I was not wholly free every time I rode the trolley to the hospital. But I had free afternoons and woke up in my own bed. It's the little things that count, I wrote in one of my poems. At that moment, daily therapy was exactly what I needed, and it was certainly no small thing.

Many people imagine that once you're in an open ward, the only way forward is home. Professionally, leaving is called being discharged, which still sounds bizarre today. "Mr. Tomc, if everything goes well, you will be discharged tomorrow. Thank you for being so cooperative, and I hope we never see each other again." It sounds ridiculous, but that is precisely what it is. The open ward is an intermediate stop. A limbo. Which means you can also go back to the closed ward. And I did. At least once. The psychiatrist didn't give me permission for a weekend break in Portorož.

It's partly my fault because I could have kept quiet, gone on a weekend getaway, and driven to the coast. It was not the best idea, as driving (it would be a relatively long drive) under the influence of strong medications is not recommended at all. Besides, I was still quite unstable, and the question was whether a potentially wild weekend might launch me back to the heights. At any rate, being a man who rarely lies, I told the doctor the truth, and she made the right decision. I erupted that evening and started shouting in the corridor that I was going home. The medical technician tried to calm me down and explained what would happen if I didn't give in. But I didn't. Following the old partisan saying "He who perseveres wins," I continued my monologue while packing my bags. Suddenly two more technicians appeared. They each took me under one arm, and off we went. Instead of Portorož, I ended up back in the closed ward—a clear victory.

As long as I was comfortable socializing with people, I spent most of my free time in the log cabin. There's always something going on, and as long as you're in the right mood, you don't care who you talk to or the conversation topic. There's no shortage of the latter. I've never had debates like those in the cabin, which is the center of the action in the Ljubljana psychiatric hospital. Ideas for projects were thrown around. The world was saved. We laughed at our ideas and encouraged each other to make it through until we were discharged.

In the evening, when the log cabin closed and we went to our wards, the action moved to the balconies and, in the wards that didn't have balconies, to the smoking rooms. As I usually had a computer (electronics are allowed in open wards), I was the center of the action. As I also had mobile Internet and a nice collection of films I downloaded on weekend trips, there was something to listen to or watch almost every night. The ward had a television, but the new movies attracted a bigger audience. And we could smoke while watching. I usually continued my movie night in my room when the lights in the corridors went out and the department door was locked. Before that, I bought a snack from a vending machine in the basement, a stone's throw from the reception office. When my visitors didn't bring them.

There's an anecdote related to the vending machine. A lovely girl was working at the basement reception office. When I went in for coffee or snacks, she always greeted me and asked me how I was doing. Sometimes we had a short conversation, and then we went our separate ways.
Well, I went my way, and she returned to whatever she was doing. But one day, she told me that she had changed jobs, and she slipped the key to the vending machine into my hand. Anyone with experience with vending machines knows that a key is a real luxury because you can refill it anytime, and you don't have to carry coins with you, which run out quickly. But the key has not only made my life in the hospital easier. When I was discharged for the last time in mid-2015, I hung it on my key chain, where it still hangs as a reminder of times I no longer want to relive. Whenever I hold the keys in my hands, it reminds me of the past. At the same time, it lets me know that I have a bright future ahead of me. But only if I never use it again.

JAKA TOMC

Remission

:):

When people find out I have bipolar disorder, one of their first questions is whether I am manic or depressed at that moment. They may be disappointed when I tell them I'm mostly somewhere in between. Professionally, this is called remission, which means a temporary health improvement. Everyone experiences remission in their way, depending on what kind of person they are. I can speak for myself, but I cannot say that something applies universally. Therefore, I ask you not to take everything you read in this chapter as absolute truth but as my remission experience. But that doesn't mean no one else experiences it the same way as I do.

While writing this book, I am in the eighth year of my freedom. The last time I got out, I swore I would last five years. Okay, I said it before, and it didn't work out. But this time it did, and I added another five years to the first goal. If I made it through five years, I could last ten. And if I make it to a decade without hospitalization in 2025, I can reasonably believe I can control it for the rest of my life.

After reading the previous paragraph, an untrained observer might conclude that I've had a great time these past seven years and that I'm such a good captain that I can easily steer the ship through the rocks that life throws at me. It's not true. Yes, I am the captain of my boat. It can't be any other way. The rocks are everywhere, and I navigate among them as best possible. But if I said I do all this quickly and without difficulty, I would be lying. Hardly a day goes by that I don't have a battle with myself. Memories from the past keep coming back to me. I'm constantly struggling with scenarios that could happen in the future. Sometimes I'm afraid I'll be shattered into a thousand pieces, even though I know the medicines are the glue that holds me together. Sometimes I feel alone, even if I'm rarely truly alone. I feel misunderstood, tired, and scared of things I had not considered. I don't feel good about my body. I don't experience emotions the way I used to. Sometimes I feel nothing, and sometimes I feel everything at once. I'm broken. I'm vegetating instead of living. This, dear reader, is my remission. The stagnation that never ends.

How do I cope? It's hard, but somehow I manage. First and foremost, my life became orderly. At the end of 2015, Neja entered my then-unstable bubble. She brought the beautiful and calm energy I needed the most at that time. After many years, I have put down roots again. After a while, life as a couple brought a particular routine, which was upgraded when our son was born. Someone once told me that a child is the ultimate grounding. He was right. But he said nothing about the stress, the worries, the sleepless nights, and the constant fear that your child will end up as a complete spoiled brat or a psychopath. So I am firmly rooted, but at the same time, I'm constantly being eaten away by something. At this point, I regret not going ahead with the relaxed people's association we set up (and even tried to register) during one of my manias.

I mentioned routine. This is the key to disease management. Of course, there is also appropriate medication, psychotherapy, understanding of your loved ones, and self-observation. But routine has brought my life back into a bubble where I feel okay. Why did I settle for okay? Because I've accepted that I'll probably never feel great, perfect, or fantastic again. Because I know that feeling good is the threshold at which the traffic light turns yellow. But let me put it another way. Okay is the safe choice. Okay is neither good nor bad. It's my open ward—the eye of the storm. The world may be crashing down around me, but nothing can get to me as long as I'm okay. My psychotherapist is horrified when I tell her I'm okay. But I've reconciled myself that in a world where seven out of ten is the upper limit, great cannot exist.

Routine is, therefore, crucial for living as normally as possible with bipolar disorder. On the other hand, routine is slowly but steadily killing me. I used to be quite spontaneous back when I didn't have a diagnosis. Relaxed, if you like. The mania reinforced this spontaneity, and I got to the point that when I left the flat, all I knew was that something good would happen. And it usually did. No plan, no goals, and no agreement on who I would meet that day. Total freedom.

Routine is the opposite of spontaneity. Of course, you can be spontaneous even within predetermined events, but those who have experienced both know there is no comparison. Today I need to know what's going to happen during the day, sometimes even what's going to happen during the week. Some of the worst things are unannounced visits. Calls from friends or just phone calls in general (I can't prepare for a live conversation). Or a spontaneous suggestion to go on a trip somewhere. Of course, this suggestion doesn't usually come out of my mouth. In short, on the one hand, I like my/our day to be planned. On the other hand, I hate myself for not being more spontaneous. Sometimes I say (out loud) that I want more spontaneity in my life, but I do nothing to break the routine that suffocates me. It's a problem that seems simple, but it's multilayered and very probably has to do with the fact that, in my mind, spontaneity has become inextricably linked to mania, which, I must stress again, I no longer want.

I have told people several times that remission is one big bunch of nothing. I have experienced it like that more than once. If you're wondering why I didn't create anything between 2011, when *Dandy Dildo* was published, and 2015, when I presented my poetry collection, the answer is: because I was in remission. At least officially. There was a period in between, about a year and a half long if I'm not mistaken, when I was like a zombie. I threatened my psychiatrist that I would stop taking all my medication if she didn't find a more appropriate therapy.

This is how a friend of mine saw one of the most distressing periods of my life and described her experience in this article:

When we went for coffee, he spoke slowly, his gaze drifting to the street. "I can't look at you for long, you know. These drugs are making me numb. My eyes are just slipping away. And the worst thing is, I can't write. I have no imagination, no inspiration," he said, distressed. We encouraged him to persevere because it would undoubtedly get better when they found the right mix of medicines. He did not persist, and after a few months, he stopped the medication.

So I stuck to my word and gave in to fate. It spread its wings, and soon we flew into the sky again.

JAKA TOMC

Internal Affairs

:):

I have outlined some of my manic episodes. You probably find the events described interesting, but you still don't know what was happening in my head during them, how it all looked through my eyes. What was buzzing around in my brain as everyday trifles were being pieced together into a fantastic story that only I could perceive in that way. So it's time to look inside me and offer you this most intimate part of me, which has remained only mine over the years when I have told my stories.

Some say they feel like gods during the manias. I can only nod to that because I've felt like that myself. I don't know what gods think and feel, just like I don't know what snow tastes like in the Himalayas. But I know how I felt when I thought I was an incarnate deity. I'll try to describe it in the most polite language possible. I hope I'll succeed.

How is divinity felt? What is it like to walk down the street thinking you are something greater? That you're not human? In one word: strange. But you get used to it. And that's the problem—accepting a different, abnormal state. When I felt that I was no longer an ordinary human being, I was overwhelmed by a mixture of feelings. First joy, happiness, pride, then fear, loneliness, sadness, and finally anger, sometimes rage. When I felt divinity for the first time, I cried. I dare say that this is a normal reaction because it's a beautiful feeling. I felt a slight fear when my brain switched back on after a few seconds. What now? What am I going to do with what I've become? Do I have any superpowers? Why me? What if I don't deserve it? When will I meet others like me? Are there others, or am I the only one?

All this was going through my head. As you can see, I didn't think I was a deity. I knew I was. I was not hallucinating. I was not standing in the middle of Mount Olympus or wherever talking to other gods. No. I was sitting in a chair in my room, and it hit me. You may remember your first orgasm. I do. I felt something then that I'd never felt before. It's hard, impossible to describe in words. So I can only say that it was stunning.

I've been many things in my manic delusions, but I've always remained me to a certain extent. I didn't think I was the Messiah when I woke up. It evolved during the day. As I mentioned before, I played a lot. So I was aware that I couldn't teleport, that I was not a member of the intergalactic police, that I was not a soldier, a dragon, or an angel, and that I could not move clouds with a wave of my hand. But in those moments, I couldn't stop. Part of me fell entirely into the movie playing in my head. The other part was aware all the time that it wasn't real. Although I always thought I was hallucinating and told others I was experiencing hallucinations, I realized while writing these lines that it wasn't quite like that. But it's indeed easier to tell someone that you had a hallucination than to explain that you saw something more in everyday things, even though part of you knew that you were not looking at anything unusual.

Sometimes, during my hikes around Ljubljana, I found myself in places I would never have gone otherwise. For example, behind the altar of the cathedral. Not on the altar, behind the altar. I walked down a corridor, which I saw for the first time then, and came to a small prayer room. For the faithful, it's probably a perfectly normal place, accessible to all, but I felt like Indiana Jones in the escape room. I looked around a little and found a lot of interesting objects. Behind me was a gold-plated sphere of some kind. I opened it and found something I no longer remember, but at the time, it was a sign that I had come into the room with a purpose. I hope I didn't take any relics out of the cathedral.

Taking and leaving objects was a frequent leisure activity in my manias. More leaving than taking, but I did borrow some things. I often left books, mostly my own, in various places. I left a book on a city bus once, then wrote and sent a text message with a clue rotating on the screens inside this and other buses. When I went out in the evening, I filled my bag or rucksack with various items and gave them to people. It made me feel good to give things away. I remember paying a taxi driver with a wristwatch worth at least twenty times the fare. I wanted to give a camera to someone I was seeing for the first time that day. Yes, that was the one worth a thousand euros. Why? Because it made me happy to think I could brighten someone's day. If not with an expensive camera, then with a little something. As a result, stuff disappeared, and when things stabilized,

I missed them. The young man didn't take the camera, but I "lost" it a few days later in one of Ljubljana's nightclubs.

Wastefulness is one of the most typical symptoms of mania. Some people take out loans, some spend all their savings, others borrow from friends or parents, and some steal. Which category do I fall into? The second and the third. In almost every mania, I have squandered everything I had at my disposal. I borrowed from my parents or found another way when I ran out. So when I ran out of money for coffee, I went to a nearby fountain, jumped in, and picked up some change. I never begged, but I did sell a painting that a friend had given me and got ten euros for it. I told the woman who bought it that the gorilla from the movie *Congo* drew it. Lucy. It seemed she believed me, and I can only hope the picture is hanging somewhere today, brightening the days of those who look at it. Did I believe that a gorilla had painted the picture? Short answer: yes. At one point, I thought I was holding a treasure. So why did I settle for a tenner? Because I needed ten euros and nothing more. I almost always took a certain amount of money with me at the beginning of the day and decided that I had to spend it that day. Sometimes it was ten euros, and sometimes it was a hundred. I ate in the best restaurants in Ljubljana and drank wine with the bums in the city park. I didn't care. All that mattered was to live the story of that day.

One early morning (manic mornings are usually exceptionally early), I went around the city center, looking for a place that would serve coffee. The cafés were still closed, and in some of them, I was turned around and told that they were not open yet and could not make me coffee. It's a good enough reason for a manic person to lose it. I'm not saying that every heavyweight who shows up at the door at seven on a Saturday morning should be served. But I am saying that sometimes a kind word, if not a cup of freshly brewed intoxicating drink, could have prevented many incidents. I wasn't thrown into overdrive then, but it did cross my mind that I had to do something about it. I paid for ten coffees in three different cafés with directions that they were to be served to those who wanted them. At the same time, they should mention that Jaka Tomc was paying for them.

I never found out whether the guests got their coffees, nor did I care. What mattered was that I'd somehow shut the servers' mouths and made a few people happy, albeit strangers. The epilogue of that morning was that I lost my bank card, my Kindle, and probably something else during my hike. But when you lose something during a manic phase, you don't focus on the loss because you know that someone has found your stuff, and you're sure they'll make good use of it. Well, maybe I was somewhat bothered about the bank card. Even when I'm manic, I like to keep that for myself.

The previous example was moderate regarding the amount of money *wasted*. You see, in mania, no amount of money goes to waste. Someone gives, and someone else gets. And I used to be an absolute master of this fantastic exchange of money and goods.

Did you know I drew all the media attention twice at

a charity event? It was an auction put on by One Eyed, a society of photographers who raised money for blind and partially sighted children every year by selling their photos. I first attended the auction in 2009 as a journalist covering the event. At some point, I saw an opportunity to shine. I didn't have to do anything other than raise my hand and say, "Eight hundred euros!" All heads in the room turned toward the origin of those three words. The camerapersons, who had already taken the statement of the mayor of Ljubljana—he had offered 750 euros for one of the photos—and were putting away their equipment, sighed and started to take their cameras out of their bags again. I didn't care about the statements and the media attention. I did it for one reason and one reason only: because I wanted to take advantage of a rare opportunity to outdo a millionaire in his field. The showdown wasn't perfect, as the mayor had already left, but even if he hadn't, I imagine he was probably too smart to get into a direct fight with a maniacal auction bidder.

I placed bids a few more times that evening and took home a grand worth of photos. I was overjoyed and proud. I knew I had done something good, although my main motive was purely egotistical. But isn't it better to give a thousand euros to charity than to throw it into a poker game? And I got some beautiful photographs, some of which I passed around and some of which I threw over the balcony.

What was very important in this story, which continued a year later, was that I had money. How I got it can be a very short story or a very long one. Let's put it this way: I sold my car.

I bought two computers for half the money. I edited videos then, and having a desktop and a laptop made sense. Since we were working on Apple computers, I decided to buy a Mac. Two of them. And some accessories. I soon sold the first one to a colleague; the second one served me well for a couple of years, then flew over the balcony, along with my photos.

In February 2010, I was at the *crime scene* again. That's when shit got real. Sponsors joined in, and the most generous bidder took home some prizes, including three months of driving a new BMW and a weekend retreat for two on the Slovenian coast. Remember my ill-fated holiday? Well, then, you already know who the big winner of that auction was. I didn't follow the strategy of the first year but let the mayor bid four figures for a single photo for the first time in the auction's history. He ate the cherry, but the cake was mine. I was no longer the likable stranger but the bidder the auctioneer glanced at during every round to see if he would raise number nine. I kept raising it until I had twelve photographs in my account, totaling 1,740 euros. Out of the 8,500 euros we raised for blind and partially sighted children, I contributed more than a fifth. I felt phenomenal. Never before or since have I basked in such attention as I did that evening. I walked away like Robin Hood winning the archery tournament. The only problem was I was shooting with borrowed arrows. Except I didn't know whom I had borrowed them from. . . .

Vest.si journalist Jaka Tomc, who donated the most money to help blind and visually impaired children this year, concluded, "It's a good cause with a great idea for photographers to donate money to help blind and visually impaired children. So I'm happy to contribute." (source: Dnevnik.si)

The attention soon disappeared. The three months of using the car were up. As I already said, the weekend package had yet to be used, and I still had to pay for the photos I had bought, at least most of the cost. In mid-July, I received a message from the organizer asking me to settle my debt or prepare for a media lynching. Of course, people talk, and even though I borrowed the money and settled the debt, the damage was done. I paid a heavy price, not only in cash, for short-term fame and my ego. I had become a crook. The one who cashed in the rewards, did the promotion, and got out. A scoundrel. A cheat. A no-good. Of course, in my mania, it didn't affect me as much as it did a few months later, when I was depressed and regretting my decisions. It was time to atone for my sins again. The bills were on the table, and I was sitting there all alone.

Some Assorted Highlights

:):

Some events have entirely escaped my memory. Not just events—months and years. If someone asked me what I was doing in 2012, I couldn't tell them much. So I asked friends, acquaintances, former colleagues, and others to share my adventures. Some of their testimonies filled in the holes in my mind like pieces of a vast jigsaw puzzle, but some of the events they described I cannot remember, no matter how hard I try.

I remember that once, when you were taken to the hospital, your mother called me, and all your friends were calling each other about who had seen you last. I went to a pub to ask and rang the bell at your home. All the lights were on; the door was locked, and no answer from you. We didn't know where you were or if something had happened to you. A couple of hours later, we found out you were in Polje. I was pretty relieved that you were "safe."

I think I vaguely remember that episode, but it may have been another one. I know I once joked that everyone now had everyone's phone numbers, and I thought it was a crazy good thing at the time.

My neighbor has, willingly or unwillingly, experienced quite a few of my episodes.

You came to my place many times, but I feared you. Later I got it, and I wasn't scared anymore. But my friends were terrified. I wanted to tell them, but your eyes were different. Your gaze was wild. You came across the field with black nails. You put a knight's banner out of the window and shouted my name at the top of your voice.

A former colleague told me an interesting story that I don't remember. He doesn't know whether it happened or not, as he was not there in person. It seems like a thing I would have done, although my manic marches have sometimes taken on an entirely new form after they have traveled via a few mouths and ears.

I heard you once lost your computer in a bar because you decided you had something urgent to explain to Pahor [prime minister at the time], and you went looking for him barefoot through the window. . . .

Now and then, I did something nice. Here's what one of my colleagues wrote about our joint holiday in Polje in 2015.

I was sitting on a bench with my sister, who was visiting me. You walked past us and gave my sister a signed copy of Manic Poet. *We chatted a little more together,*

I don't remember what, and then you went on your way.

There are many stories from manic periods. But those from depressive ones, or periods when I was under the influence of solid drugs, are much fewer.

What I remember the most is that you had thick, white saliva collecting in the corners of your mouth. And that you were just a shadow of a stable Jaka. You were stable then, but we felt you were at 60 percent speed. That everything was uphill. And it seemed to me like it was all very tiring for you. But you didn't give up.

I couldn't describe the process of crawling out of the abyss any better. Saliva in the corners of your mouth, like a horse pulling a heavy load. Steady, but slowed down—just the opposite of mania. The last sentence reminded me of something a good friend once wrote.

I got goosebumps all over my body when I realized how strong a person must be to be going through what you're going through. To keep going and taking these small steps, despite all these leaps backward. To fight. To persevere. And to learn through this challenging and thorny journey.

JAKA TOMC

A Single Night Can Change Everything

:):

Sleeping. The most important part of the day for every human being. During sleep, our cells regenerate; brain cells even reorganize as they make new connections and let go of some old ones. The heart rate slows down, body temperature drops slightly, and growth hormones are released (causing body growth in children and, for example, nail and hair growth in adults). Lack of sleep has undesirable consequences, such as tiredness, irritability, and poorer concentration. Long-term sleep deprivation has been linked to overweight, diabetes, cardiovascular disease, high blood pressure, and premature death.

For a bipolar person, quality sleep—and the right amount of it—is priority number one! This applies to both manic and depressive phases. Sleep deprivation experiments in depressed people illustrate the power of sleep. One study found that depression symptoms in about half of the participants *improved* after they were kept awake for one night. Sounds great, but after a night's sleep, 50 percent to 80 percent of these people fell back into depression.

One night is enough to change everything. In manic phases, you don't sleep much, just a few hours daily. I used to wake up at three or four in the morning, or I would be awake through the night and compensate during the day. Sometimes I dozed off for a few minutes in the restroom at work. Sometimes I put on my sunglasses and napped on the pub terrace. Human ingenuity is infinite, and sleep is essential. But when you are manic, other things seem more important than sleep. You want to experience as much as possible. You want to squeeze every last drop out of every single day. But days are too short, so you extend them into nights and sometimes new mornings. Sleep deprivation lifts you even more. You compensate for tiredness with an excess of energy, which you can use only by moving, talking, dancing, running, and jumping. And you don't get that at home. I didn't. That's why, during every mania, I spent days wandering around Ljubljana, looking for things to do. And when you're manic, a trivial thing can become a glorious event.

If sleep deprivation is typical in mania (and as far as I know, it is), then it would be logical to conclude that the opposite is true in depression—that there is excessive sleep. That is both true and false. I've already mentioned one of my depressive episodes in which I was plagued by insomnia. That's also the one that sticks in my mind the most because it was distressing. In general, however, I agree with the excessive-sleep hypothesis. Since I had neither the desire nor the will nor the strength to do anything, I spent most of the day lying down and most of it sleeping. I'm talking about depressions during which I had no work. It was very different when I had to go to the office; at those times, the depressions were shorter and less intense.

As much as the work woke me up from my numbness in a way, the desire to sleep was ever-present. The awakenings were the most terrible. I read a post online where a mother talked about her child waking up every morning saying, "Help, I'm awake!" I could quickly identify. That's precisely what it was like for me every morning of depression. When I opened my eyes, I first looked at the clock and hoped it was two in the morning. Of course, it never was. It was usually five minutes before the alarm rang. "No, no!" or something even juicier often came out of my mouth, and I thought the same thing as the boy in the post. *Help, I'm awake!*

In my normal state, I am a person who likes to sleep. I also like to be awake, but I have no need to sacrifice sleep in favor of other night activities, although sometimes I am chronically short of time for all my projects. I am also no stranger to afternoon naps. Now and then, I doze after lunch, sometimes for an hour or two.
I would say that I get between seven and nine hours of sleep a night.

When I was manic, I used to sleep for three to five hours. I mentioned a little earlier that sleep deprivation improves the condition of depressed people. I can confirm that. I can also conclude that a good night's sleep alleviates mania. Psychiatrists know this, which is why they prescribe drugs that affect sleep. Once, before I was diagnosed, my therapist gave me some melatonin pills. I don't remember how they affected my sleep, but she told me something later that I will never forget. "If you can't sleep, turn on the TV and drink a small can of beer." I'm saying loud and clear that I don't support excessive drinking. And I am aware that such advice can quickly escalate into uncontrolled gulping of alcohol in order to sleep. *One is none* is a phrase familiar to every Slovene and often used behind the bar and sometimes even in the shelter of the four walls of the home. Alcohol and drugs cause severe problems for too many people, and even more for bipolar ones. That's why I'm about to devote an entire chapter to them.

Ninety-Nine Bottles of Beer on the Wall

:):

Slovenians are an alcohol-drinking nation. We're proud of it, and most people like to drink. Or, to put it another way, we want to be (at least a little) drunk. A stand-up comedian once said, "I don't drink because I like the taste. No one does. We drink because we have to."

I've been drunk a lot since I was in high school. I was what you might call a social drinker. I drank when we were out and sometimes at home, just enough so I didn't arrive utterly sober at a party or social gathering. I rarely got behind the wheel drunk, and I was caught DUI only once. I'm a typical Slovene, probably a bit below average in my drinking tendencies, which is good.

Some people believe that it was alcohol, drugs, and excessive partying that triggered my bipolar disorder. My first hospitalization was in 2007, and, as I've already mentioned, a good part of that year was spent partying. But the first time I lost it was on my graduation trip to Greece, where you don't ask what the waiter put in your drink. Well, even if you do—and I did once—the amount of alcohol in a cocktail is too much in proportion to the satisfaction that washes over you when you hold the glass in your hand. I don't know about today, but that was how it was in those days. Anyway, there was always something going on in Crete, and considering what I know today, I could say that I was a bit manic.

One evening, I got into a fight with a future doctor because he wouldn't let me talk to his female classmates. It almost ended in a fistfight in the street, but it all unraveled when I started shouting at him to kill me because he would be doing me a favor. To this day, I do not know whether I was playing the psycho card or whether I was serious.

The pool party was also suspicious. Suspicious regarding my mood, because I was a bit high all the time. It could have been the alcohol, but the feelings were similar, if not identical, to those I had in my later manias. All in all, the pool party went great. Good music, dancing, and exciting discussions. Until I discovered a hotel next to the pool with a well-stocked, lone bar next to it. I strolled over, accompanied by at least one companion, sat on a bar stool, and poured myself a drink. In between, I chatted with other hotel guests, offered them drinks, and generally felt incredible. You may think that's not a big deal, but I don't usually talk to strangers. Small talk is still something that gives me the chills. Well, at twenty-five, it might have been different, but still. That scene was typical of a manic Jaka.

In a shop, I found a plastic gun that shot plastic balls. Nothing too dangerous unless you hit someone in the eye at close range. Well, I walked around with that gun that looked like a real gun, spraying "bullets" all over the place. The boat ride back was an absolute shootout, too, until a couple of people told me to calm down a bit, and I went back to doing what I usually did, which was drinking.

But I saved the most manic scene for the last night. First, outside, where I was having a beer with a colleague, I was shouting to the sky that nobody understood me and I was born at the wrong time, and asking why it had to be me. Then I burst into tears. Later, inside the ship (we went to Greece on a huge ferry), in the dining room, I shouted at the organizers and entertainment staff that they were scoundrels because they could eat on vouchers while we had to pay for the food. I also mentioned that they were there because of us and not vice versa. Well, I ended up being escorted by my classmates to my cabin, where I cried again.

The next day was beautiful again as if nothing had happened the night before. The rest of the journey was uneventful, and if anyone looked at me funny, I didn't notice. In all likelihood, my blackout was attributed to too much alcohol, so there was no resentment. You might be interested to know how the story with the med student ended. I found him at a beach party and apologized to him. He was pleased with my gesture, and so was I. I wouldn't have wanted to end up on his operating table somewhere along the line.

It's possible that alcohol was to blame for my (admittedly short-lived) episodes on the grad trip. I did not consume any drugs, apart from aspirin, which I gulped one night and found out that it made me sober. Alcohol is a bastard. In a very short time, it can reveal parts of your personality you may not even know. Or you do know them but have repressed them somewhere deep down, probably for a reason. And indeed, those sides of you are unknown to those who have never seen you drunk.

People drink for different reasons. By drinking, I mean excessive drinking, binge drinking, not the occasional consumption of small amounts of alcohol. Some people drink to forget or to dull the pain. Others drink to remember or to draw out a repressed self. I belong to the second group. Alcohol usually relaxes me, whereas in my normal state I'm pretty introverted and don't talk much. I become more talkative and open when drunk. But not always. Sometimes the effect is the opposite, and I shut down even more or have anxiety attacks. It depends on the situation and the people around me at the time. But it's almost a rule that in a drunken state, I fall asleep.
No matter where I am. I once fell asleep on the loudspeaker of a nightclub and became a worthy successor to my father, who dozed off in a well-known pizzeria while he was eating.

I always found it amusing when doctors asked me if I drank alcohol or smoked weed. Why amusing? Because, in small amounts, both have done me more good than harm, especially in mania. Pot calms me down so much that I function on a purely fundamental level. It slows me down, and I need that when I'm manic. I don't know if I've ever seen anyone bursting with energy after smoking a joint.

Unless he had something else in it, but that's another story. Let me emphasize that these are my observations and not an expert's opinion. Excessive drug use is harmful and can be fatal. The same applies to alcohol and tobacco. Therefore, I advise against experimentation, and if you're taking medication simultaneously, consult your doctor.

It's the same with alcohol. Beer or wine has had a soothing effect on me in my manias. I'm talking about one beer or one glass of wine, not all-night drinking. Spirits can be problematic because they get you high, and I'm not even going to talk about energy drinks and vodka cocktails because they burn your brain and fuck with your heart. A beer sipped slowly in a pleasant atmosphere does more to calm the mania than all the conversations with friends. Sorry, but that's the way it is. When I used to drink only nonalcoholic beer, it catapulted me so much that I couldn't find a way back. It was even worse when I drank only water and natural juices. You need something to pull you back to earth when you're not grounded (mania is very much like no longer having the floor under your feet). Once is not enough. You need it every day, several times a day. Sometimes pills are not enough. So I tell you, dear brothers and sisters, find something to keep you grounded. For some, it will be a glass of beer. For others, it will be a visit to the zoo or cinema. Do not let yourself get too high, because the fall will be harrowing.

The fact is that alcohol and drugs can push you to one extreme or the other. It happened to me. Sometimes one night was enough. One sleepless night or one sniffed line.

I can't imagine where I'd have gone if I'd tried LSD or mushrooms, especially in a manic state.

Today I drink moderately. By moderate, I mean that I sometimes have a glass of wine or a small beer at lunchtime (on weekends, not during working hours), but almost as a rule, I have a drink in the evening. One drink, make no mistake. Why, if I have just finished preaching about the dangers of alcohol? Because I'm an adult, and I know how to listen to my body. A few years ago, I asked a former psychiatrist if I could order mulled wine from the stalls in December. Her words brought a smile to my face. "Just don't have too much. There's a lot of sugar in mulled wine, which makes you fat."

There have been times when I've been overly concerned about what I put on and in myself. I've considered what I could eat, how much, what I could drink, and whether I could smoke. I know that unhealthy food is harmful and makes me gain weight. That every pack of cigarettes I smoke shortens my life by a few minutes. That a fizzy drink will not quench my thirst. But you know what? When I eat a Wiener schnitzel and fries for lunch, wash it down with sweetened bubbly water, and light up a cigarette on the balcony after, I feel like a winner. I'm indeed overweight, and I get out of breath more quickly when I walk up the stairs, but after four decades of life, I deserve to live the life that suits me. I'm entitled to it.

What Triggers Mania?

:):

I argue that mania can be identified at the right time and consequently prevented, so identifying the trigger moments is crucial. If hypomania can occur overnight or over a longer period of time, hypermania can happen instantaneously. Let's see what my triggers were.

I'm trying to remember the year, but it was probably summer or late spring. I ate out a lot because I spent practically all my days—moderately manic—on the streets of Ljubljana. It was a weekend, or I was on holiday. I sat in a restaurant's garden, where I would occasionally have a bite to eat or chat with the former owner or one of the servers. It was morning, an ideal time for a good snack. At least twice before, they'd made me scrambled eggs, even though they didn't have them on the menu. I wanted them that day too. The waiter suggested they put some asparagus inside, and I agreed. It was delicious, and I asked for the bill while sipping my coffee. Then came the surprise: I was not charged for scrambled eggs but for a frittata with asparagus. The price was double. I lost it and started to berate the waiter. I think the chef came out and tried to calm the situation, to no avail. I took a ten from my wallet and threw it on the table. "I understand," I muttered. "You're ripping off the regulars. Shame on you!" I exited the garden and started another manic march through the city.

On another occasion, I lost it because of a computer game. It was a strategy game called Erepublik, played in real time and involving real people. I met some of them, and have kept in touch with a few. In the game, on one occasion, I became president of Slovenia. It was a presidential position with many powers, unlike in real life. I had a government, control over state-owned companies, and the ability to start wars with other countries. At that point in time, I played every moment at my disposal. At work, in the afternoon at the pub, and when I should have been asleep. It was going quite well for a while, and it even looked like I would finish my one-month mandate successfully. Then the opposition came on the scene and started their plan to throw me off balance. I began to lose control over the situation in the game, and in my own body. I finished my mandate in the hospital.

There was another triggering moment linked to the game. On one occasion, in real life, I took a photo of an invoice I had issued to a company. One of the employees (I still don't know who it was) saw the photo on Facebook and took the news to the CEO, saying that I was publishing the employees' salaries. Although I was not doing that at all, the boss wasn't happy, so I stayed home that day as a precaution and tried to find out who was responsible for the situation. I discovered (or imagined) that one of the workers was playing Erepublik. I informed a few people in the game that someone was doing shit to me in real life, and I passed this information on to my employer. If the morning before I found out what was going on was relatively calm, I went completely crazy during the day. The man I had accused quit working there a few weeks later. To this day, I do not know whether I had something to do with it or whether the matter took its natural course. However, one thing did take its natural course, and they were already making my bed in Polje.

A few times, an interview or an article published about me has triggered a bout of hypermania. When you're hypomanic, any extra impulse can jump-start you. An interview in a magazine read by thousands of people can be a very effective trigger. When I read some old interviews in my normal state, I can immediately see when I was manic and when I wasn't. In 2015, as I mentioned, I published a poetry book, but the launch party was not a trigger, although some people believed so. I went into the hospital a month after the party, and mania can't last that long (at least for me). I probably became hypomanic at the party, and the actual trigger was . . . drugs. I don't remember everything I took, but there was definitely "ice cream," or 3-MMC, on the table. This synthetic drug causes extreme changes in consciousness (feelings of comfort, euphoria, warmth, love, and relaxation). Mania powder, that is. To top it all off, I was taking 5-HTP at the time, which is not a drug but a kind of natural antidepressant. All this led to an explosion of emotions that took me to a place I never want to return to.

I wrote this on one of my blogs:

Many of you are wondering why I ended up in the hospital. The answer is very simple. I'm an asshole.

I took drugs on Thursday. I mean, we had an afterparty at home. I did one line, thinking that ice cream or ice was something good. Fuck it. Coke hits me well. It seems that amphetamines don't.

Anyway, I didn't sleep for three days, and the women's eyes were so colorful I was freaking out with hormones. I loved them all. I had so much energy. Like two suns together. When I told one I would write a song about her eyes, she said, "Jaka, I love girls."

Retired at Thirty? Hell, No!

:):

After several hospitalizations and the sickness absences that followed, during one of my visits, my doctor mentioned the possibility of disability retirement. I immediately replied that I had no plans to retire; I intended to continue working and lead a fruitful life. She nodded and never mentioned the matter again.

I guess that's the protocol for a person who's on sick leave every few months. I suppose many people would be happy to accept such an offer. I've met people who have. I had different plans. I wanted to live, not just cruise through life on autopilot. The disease was at its peak, but I believed I could manage it if I couldn't overcome it. I knew I'd made the right choice when I rejected the proposal. I realized that because I was fighting an insidious disease, I was strong, not weak. Too many people had planted the idea in my head that I couldn't do it. But that afternoon in the doctor's surgery, I was more determined than ever to show them I could. Anything I put my mind to.

I don't think it's shameful to take a disability pension. It's clear to me that some people have no choice.

Others have a choice but have good reasons for taking it. For some, it's the easier route. It seemed to me at the time that I'd have closed the door on myself by making a bargain at the age of thirty. I wanted to live life to the full, even with bipolar disorder. I wanted to work, to create, to be who I am. I was miserable when I was out of work (or unable to work because of medication). Of course, not working also brings with it a lack of money, and in combination with mental illness, things can go seriously wrong very quickly.

July 31, 2017—Facebook post

How life turns around. A few years ago, I was written off and told to consider a proposal to retire on disability. I was no longer Jaka. Or Tomc. I was "the one who's bipolar" and "the one who's back in Polje." I was knocked down, tired after all the ups and downs that are expected but still surprise you with their intensity. I was broken. I was no longer Jaka. I wondered how to get out. I wished I hadn't woken up in the morning. I begged the universe to bring me back into balance.

Despite everything, I persevered. When it was the worst, writing was my salvation. That's when Dandy Dildo *was born. That's when many poems were written. That's when Jaka was born again. I decided that although the illness and I shared a body, the illness was not me, and I was not it. I talked to it (as cheesy as it sounds) and told it I would bury the hatchet. We decided to coexist.*

More than two years have passed since my last

hospitalization—a new record. In the meantime, I cut some people out of my life to make room for new ones. I had to change something. Am I sorry? No. After a long time, I'm alive again. I am thinking. I feel. I may still be "the one who was in a mental institution" for some, but for many, I'm "the one who didn't give up."

Perseverance is crucial in coping with bipolar disorder (and other illnesses). I'm not saying this is enough. The outcome is not always positive, but if you've done everything you can, you're a winner. And the feeling that you're winning is vital. I reward myself for the small victories. It could be for a work assignment, for a certain number of words written for a new story, or for selling one of my books. I can't emphasize enough—reward yourself for the small victories.

Once, a friend and I agreed that every night we would write down ten things we were grateful for that day and email them to each other. This is what one of my messages looked like.

April 10, 2011, 00:45

1. *It was so lovely during the move.*
2. *My arms hurt, but it's nice to feel alive.*
3. *I am pleasantly tired.*
4. *It's been a lovely couple of days,*
5. *very summery.*
6. *I need to tidy up my car and flat.*
7. *We ate well, we drank well.*

> 8. *My mom made me a great breakfast.*
> 9. *X has a cute single neighbor.*
> 10. *Animals love me, and I love them.*
> 11. *I was invited to the seaside.*
> 12. *I found a parking spot next to the building.*
> 13. *I realized that I need to enjoy my sick days more and worry less.*
> 14. *I realized that I can still talk.*
> 15. *I realized that I'm a relatively cool guy.*
> 16. *The day ended with a cigar on the balcony.*

Gratitude is vital, and the above correspondence influenced my getting out of an unpleasant mood earlier. When you're grateful for things, events, people, and others, you feel alive and realize that life can be beautiful again. This is essential if you want to turn the curve upward again.

The third thing that pulls you out of the abyss is creation. I wrote in *Manic Poet* that when the going gets tough, you either start creating or end up killing yourself. That there is no middle way. But that statement was too radical or lacked explanation. Creation has to be seen broadly, not necessarily as artistic expression. What I meant by creating is that you move and start doing something. A better word would be activation. You've done the central part of the business when you activate yourself by finding activities that interest you again, fill you with positive energy, and distract you from negative thoughts.

Writing has pulled me out of depression a few times. Half of the short novel *Dandy Dildo* was written in the open ward of the clinic. I was so severely depressed then that I don't understand how I could've started writing a romantic comedy. It was published the following year and is now one of my most-read books. If I couldn't write prose, I wrote poems. If I couldn't write poetry, I wrote a diary—anything to get my thoughts on paper or a computer screen. The things I wrote often seemed meaningless, boring, and irrelevant. But when I read the same texts a few months later, when I felt better, I noticed the depth and breadth of what I'd written. I had created something out of nothing, a story or a poem out of blank paper. Is there anything better than that?

JAKA TOMC

I'm going horizontal,
with slight deviations.
I turn left and right,
and a little up and down,
sometimes diagonally.
I explore the polygon of normality.
It's mysteriously unknown.
Quiet and slightly dull,
but comfortable and attractive,
varied and wide.
Sometimes I'm tempted,
to step out of my comfort zone,
to fly again,
to break the horizon,
to shoot straight up,
above the gray clouds,
to touch the sun again.
But not today.
Because I feel seven out of ten.
And that's good.
Tens are for masters,
and I'm an average student
at the University of Life
and until I pass all my exams,
I can't get a degree.

I Don't Want to Die, but I'm Tired of Living

:):

In the opening chapter, I mentioned how I theatrically swallowed a handful of pills in front of my mother. My performance aimed not to end my life but to escape that situation. I had to break the tension that had been created. To stop the flow of events, I applied the handbrake. It could have ended tragically, but fortunately, it didn't.

In mania, you usually don't think about suicide. Maybe at the end, when the gigantic manic wave breaks and you start falling. In mania, there is a much greater risk of something happening to you because you are not paying enough attention or are delusional than because you're deliberately trying to hurt yourself. In depression, it is entirely different. You're alone with your thoughts, which are dark and negative. The agony is sometimes too great, so the way out offered to you seems like a good choice.

Have I ever considered suicide? Yes and no.
I've never attempted suicide, but I've often wished I hadn't woken up in the morning. I don't know if I wanted to die as

much as I didn't want to live anymore. Maybe I was not brave enough to take the final step. Or my desire to live was too great. Whatever the case, I always somehow came to a point where I said to myself, "If I don't want to die, I want to live." That point was the turning point in every relationship I had with depression, and shortly after that, we broke up.

Another way out of depression is to realize that everything passes. I don't mean the awareness of one's transience, although that is inevitable too. I'm talking about the fact that depression will sooner or later be a thing of the past. When it will happen depends on patience, perseverance, and creation/activation (and appropriate therapy). Once you've overcome depression, don't forget to reward yourself and acknowledge how damn strong you are for having gone through it (again).

The number of episodes means nothing, so there is no point in bothering about it. However, some claim that every manic episode and every depression leaves a lasting impact on the brain. If you thought you'd waved goodbye to depression for good and it comes back after a while, don't despair. Know that you're stronger than the illness, even if it's debilitating and you see no way out. After a few hospitalizations, I stopped counting the number of times I was in. I think the hospital stopped counting too. The discharge slip from the beginning of 2011 says that I was admitted to the hospital for the fifth time in September 2010, and the one from 2013 just says that I was admitted.

I'm trying to say that I had many reasons to surrender. Every time the nurses in the admissions ward welcomed me (actually, it was like, "Tomc, what are you doing here again?"), my world crumbled into dust. I took every hospitalization as a personal defeat. I didn't like coming back. You might think that nobody wants to, but that's not true. Some people go to the hospital to escape a life that doesn't spare them. I was not one of them. Every time they clipped my wings and put me back in the abyss with the help of drugs, my morale plunged. Every time I was released back into the wild, I promised myself it would be the last time. But it never was. Sometimes I lasted a few years, sometimes a few days. I've often settled into a fetal position at home and let the suffering take me over completely. Maybe that wasn't a wrong decision because I reached the bottom faster, and then the only way was—you guessed it—up.

JAKA TOMC

Bucket List

:):

Do you want to know what a manic person desires? Let's look at the ten things I added to my bucket list in April 2013 and published on my former blog with the meaningful title *Bipolar Times*.

1. *Write a good book and sell a million copies.*
2. *Meet Zach Braff and hug him.*
3. *Write a script. Act in the movie.*
4. *Slap Damjan Murko [a Slovene singer], then pay him with a beer and a hug.*
5. *Write a song for a famous music group.*
6. *Meet Justin Bieber. Hug him, then kick him in the balls.*
7. *Buy a beach house in Cuba.*
8. *Learn Portuguese.*
9. *Get one million hits on this blog by the end of the year.*
10. *Get a knight's armor and a sword. Get kitted up and walk the streets of Ljubljana.*

I described the list as not too utopian and optimistically predicted that half of the wishes would be realized by the end of the year. Three guesses on how many ticks I made . . .

My hypomanic wishes were, to put it mildly, far-fetched. During full-blown mania, they bordered on madness. I remember that in one of my last manias, in 2015, I dreamt that I could discover the secret of bipolar disorder and even win a Nobel Prize for my work. I took the project seriously, writing down my findings, a little in a notebook, a little on a computer, and drawing a kind of diagram on a blackboard in the kitchen of my apartment. My ambitious project was interrupted by hospitalization. When I came home a few weeks later for a weekend outing, I looked at the board and couldn't understand anything. The diagram made no sense. I felt like the psychiatrist the psychology professor in high school told us about, the one who tried peyote. Suddenly "everything" became clear to him, and the typical reaction was to write it down. If I remember correctly, he wrote it on the wall. The next day he realized that the writing was meaningless. Well, at that moment, I felt like that scientist. I put the Nobel Prize behind me and returned to the grayness of everyday life.

When I published my first book, I said in an interview that I would sell more books in Slovenia than Dan Brown. At that time, I had 100,000 copies in mind. I didn't know that this was not only a vast number but practically unattainable. But I went even further. I had already planned the translations of the book, so I predicted that I could crush the Bible. On a global scale, of course. That was in 2010, and some six billion copies of the Bible had been sold worldwide by then. Six billion. My exact answer to the question of whether I could achieve the fame of a character in my book was this:

I can even surpass it if I reach the fame of Dan Brown, which means 80 million on a global scale. But I want to sell a billion of them. If they've sold six billion copies of the Bible, why shouldn't I sell a billion? The Americans buy everything anyway. I will launch the book in China, India, the Balkans, and Australia. The world is a big place. People are just scared and happy if they sell 200 copies. I'll be glad when everyone has one of mine in their home.

My ideas were obviously very ambitious. I might even have had the book translated into Mandarin if I hadn't been stopped. Many people probably thought I was a windbag for saying things like that. I'm not too offended by that, but I do care. It's also true that at my first press conference, I said I would be the Dennis Rodman of Slovenian literature. I even described Goran Vojnović (an awarded Slovene writer) as an ideal son-in-law. Today, I'm not a bad boy in the Slovenian literary scene, and I don't deal with other writers very much except by reading their work.

I officially became a writer in 2010 when I published the first part of my novel *Zgodba o Davidu Locku* (*The David Locke Story*). Few people know why I started writing. The answer will surprise most. I was inspired to write by Hank Moody. Who? The main character of *Californication*. I watched the series and said, "This is it." A few days later, I wrote the first chapter on my computer at work. The next day I continued. And the day after that. I wrote and wrote and wrote until they got me. They offered me two options.

I could stay with them and do my job (which didn't involve writing a book), or I could resign and write books. I decided, as a manic person should, to choose the life of a writer.

For the first years of my life with bipolar disorder, I had no book-related cravings. But I had desires as well as goals and ideas. The wish of all wishes was born a few days before I went into the hospital for the first time. When asked what I wanted for Christmas, I replied, "Peace on earth." From that moment on, I understand the beauty queens of our planet. I'm sure some of them say it out of habit or because they think it's the right thing to do. I was dead serious. Tears were rolling down my cheeks when I said those three famous words. I had the ultimate wish, which would probably be unrealizable for some time. But maybe, who knows, when I made that wish, the world was at peace, if only for a second or a minute. We'll never know.

As you can see, my wishes weren't bad or harmful (apart from kicking Justin Bieber in the balls)—peace on earth, good book sales, and a beach house. I know people with whom there's nothing wrong (at least not that I know of), and they have even greater desires than mine. Perhaps I've learned over the years not to dream big. For Slovenians, modesty is an attractive trait. So I've also learned to be modest, work, and desire as little as possible. Because, let's face it, it would've turned out much better if someone else had starred in the film based on my book.

Since 2010, my aspirations have been more or less related to writing. I want to write for a living.

I've never hidden that. After many years without any severe episodes, I realize it's a long run and, above all, hard work. But, indeed, you never know which book will give you that much-needed breakthrough that launches you into stardom. In sports, they say that talent is ten percent, and the rest is training. It's the same with writing or any other field. There's a bunch of people who want to write a book. I do not doubt that some of them would write a great book. But in the end, what distinguishes writers from theoretical writers is that they sit at a computer and write. The text in my head is worth as much as my manic desires.

December 2012—Facebook post

I want to become immortal. Mentioned in history books. I want to become one of the greatest writers ever.

I once told a colleague in the elevator that I would write a book explaining everything. A few years later, I wrote that line in *Manic Poet*. The book explained some things, but not everything, just as this book won't. Or any other. You can never explain everything. That has become crystal clear to me over the years. But I had a fixed idea that day that one day in the future, I would write the book of all books. Once I thought I would publish a book called *Eleven Days*, which would refer to the eleven days of being strapped to a bed in 2010. It would've been a blank book. Crazy idea? In 2016, Shed Simove published *What Every Man Thinks About Apart From Sex*. There are 200 blank pages in it. The book became a bestseller and was translated (yes, you read that right) into many languages, including Slovenian.

Perhaps I should listen to myself more and consider my wishes, even if I sometimes call them sick.

It's funny that at the end of my first book, it says that if I had to describe myself in a hundred thousand words, I would write a book. None of my books has a hundred thousand words, and I doubt any will. Maybe I want to tell you everything about myself, but instead of writing a single book, I'll reveal myself throughout the whole oeuvre. Maybe one day, I'll publish all my stories in one giant book called *The Jaka Tomc Story*. Probably not.

Why Be Normal?

:):

September 10, 2017—blog post

"People who say they are not bothered by your mental illness are not bothered by your mental illness as long as you don't behave like a person with a mental health condition." —Matt Haig

I did not set out to be bipolar. I didn't ask for it. At least, I don't think I did. I always wanted to be unique. That wish has come true for me. With a blood type of O negative, I'm in the eighth percentile of the population. As a bipolar, I'm in the second to third percentile, and as a writer, poet, and publisher, I'm in an even narrower group. So I am, without a shadow of a doubt, exceptional.

I was told to be normal many times in my life. I've never answered with the trite "What is normal, anyway?" I usually answered with "Why?" Why be normal? I've never been, and I never want to be. I don't think I'm cut out for something great, even though I'm a Leo by zodiac, and I like success. Life gives you one chance. Will you waste it on being normal? To be like other people? Or will you be bold, find your path, and walk it, even though people will try to get you off it because it isn't normal?

We're all different. For some, normality suits them. Not for me. It's not a pose. It's just who I am. I decided to write when I had to decide whether to keep my job or write books. That's not normal. Not in Slovenia. Just like it wasn't normal that I learned to read before I got rid of the baby bottle. That I knew how to write while I was still peeing in bed. But it was normal that I didn't skip a grade in primary school because I was supposedly too childish. It's normal for a child to be a mature individual at the age of seven, not playing with toy cars.

Speaking of mature specimens—it's only with them that normality, or the lack of it, becomes apparent. Immediately after the first contact, we can declare someone normal or abnormal. Whether it's because of their physical appearance, the clothes they wear, the sentences they form, or their general behavior. Questions about their job, family, home location, and leisure activities give us enough information to put them in the appropriate box of normality. It's then up to us whether we open that drawer again or leave it closed because it doesn't suit us.

I don't mind not being normal. But it bothers me that it bothers some other people. It's not because I'm upset about what other people think. We should all realize that an abnormality leads to crucial shifts in all areas. Can you name one person who has made a fundamental mark on human history and claimed they were normal? Probably not. So don't try to be normal, even if people tell you to. Discover your talents, develop them, and be who you are.

Above all, walk your path alone or with people close to you. You are not normal. No one is. Normal *is just a word that cannot be defined. But you are defined. One way or another.*

JAKA TOMC

On the Couch

:):

As I cannot rely on my memory (especially for particular years), I had to dig up this information from old emails. I've been going to psychotherapy since November 14, 2013. At the time of writing this book, I see my therapist once a month, but there have been times when I've seen her every week. It just depends on my condition. It is self-pay psychotherapy. I also tried a therapist the public health service assigned to me, but we didn't click, so I stopped going after a few sessions. The current one suits me perfectly, which is probably logical and goes without saying, given the length of time we've been working together.

I don't remember the first meeting, but it was a getting-to-know-you session. I remember her saying that after about five or six meetings, we would see if we were a good match. I loved it. I realized then that in her eyes, I was not just a number that would bring in fresh dough now and then. I would have ended our story after two months if we hadn't been a match. Nobody can help everyone, so this is the only right and fair thing to do.

How did I get to her in the first place? She was recommended to me by a former psychiatrist.

I'm eternally grateful to her for that. Well, and to myself for having the courage to write to her. Because many people still see psychotherapy as something we people with mental health conditions need, but others don't. Of course, that's not the case. We should make it compulsory for every adult to have a few sessions. If anyone anywhere is at peace with themselves, has no traumas or fears, and is satisfied with the world surrounding them and their role in it, then I congratulate them on that and bow deeply to them. To everyone else, I recommend an occasional dose of psychotherapy.

I do remember one of our initial meetings. She asked me about my childhood. I said it was happy. That my parents had raised me to be an honest man, and I was grateful to them. Well, she said, "Now we can begin." That was it. The beginning of several years of dancing in which we tried out different music and dance styles. I don't know if there's any problem we didn't address. She draws answers out of me in different ways—by drawing, writing, visualizing, exercising, and, most of all, talking.

I'd be lying if I said that I looked forward to our time together every time. Many times, especially in depressive periods, I thought I wouldn't say a thing. A few times, I was lying on the sofa at home until the last moment when I had to leave home so I wouldn't be late. Other times I would have a glass of wine or a beer at a nearby pub to relax a bit before my appointment. I've also canceled a session because I didn't feel like talking. I consider all this to be normal behavior.

I don't know about other therapists and their modus operandi, but I like that we don't go for classical psychotherapy. I don't know if it looks like in the movies, where the patient drones on and the therapist takes notes (or scribbles something in his notebook). With my therapist, sessions mainly consist of dialogue, and the approach is holistic. I already mentioned that we touch on all topics, including energies, meditation, and grounding. I feel better after each session than I did before. That is essential—that psychotherapy doesn't exhaust me (although sometimes it does) but gives me a new impetus.

It's easy to conclude from all the above that I recommend psychotherapy. It's helped me immeasurably. I cannot imagine where and what I would be today if my therapist and I had realized at the end of 2013 that we were not a good match.

JAKA TOMC

A Landmark Year

:):

The year 2015 was an important one in many ways. I published my first (and, at the time of this writing, only) collection of poetry—*Little Pleasures*. There were so many people at the launch party that, despite my mild mania, I panicked and managed to read only one poem, and they practically forced me to do it. The applause I received after the reading was so thunderous that I can still hear it today. I regret not using the evening better, but it had to be that way. That was on March 12. On St. Gregory's Day. Exactly one month later, I was taken away. At that point, I stopped counting how many times I'd been in. There was no point. I probably didn't break any records, but I killed my hope of being normal again.

A renowned psychiatrist once told me that every mania leaves a mark on the brain. Combined with the atrophy mentioned earlier, with which I was diagnosed when I was still a beginner bipolar, I must have hit the jackpot. My brain was dying, and I had to awkwardly smile, nod, participate in conversations with other plebeians (and sometimes aristocrats), and pretend that I was okay. I shouldn't have to do that, but since society has taught me over the years not to feel sorry for myself (and, by inference, not for others), I've also mastered pushing my thoughts and feelings deep down inside. Even today, I don't tell anyone when I have occasional anxiety attacks. It's probably not right, and I don't know why I do it, but that's the way it is. But it is one of the things I'd like to change and will change soon. I prefer that anxiety leave me alone, but I'll save that wish for some other occasion.

In the spring of 2015, my life was beautiful. The *Little Pleasures* were selling well, and I was again wandering around Ljubljana's cafés and nightclubs, brimming with positive energy. This time it wasn't as wild as eight years earlier, although ... I was hospitalized in mid-April. I don't remember what the trigger was. I was in the hospital for less than a month. That sounds like a lot, but it's very acceptable. I told the psychiatrist I had decided to take five years of peace and stability, so I wouldn't be back in the hospital for five years. At that time, it sounded and looked realistic. I picked myself up quite differently from the previous episodes. Each time I'd been knocked from the heights to the bottom of the pit, I'd spent months (or even years) gluing myself together. Not then. When I left the hospital, I was still a bit high. The medication did slow me down, but not enough. There was drinking, singing, and dancing again. I was everywhere. I took the pills when I took them, sometimes before I went out, sometimes at five in the morning. New acquaintances were made, and old ones were dropped. We were closing pubs and opening cafés in the morning. Sometimes I didn't even go to bed. Sometimes I thanked a higher power that I didn't fall asleep at the wheel in the middle of the highway. Sometimes I got a comment from friends that something was wrong again. But I trusted strangers throwing pills and powders on the table more than I trusted my longtime companions. Perhaps they were not persistent enough. Maybe that's normal. Everyone has their fuck-ups, and no time for someone who enjoys their madness too much to get their shit together. That's how I interpret it. I never asked the others about it.

I was free for a few days. I was sitting in a café on Trubarjeva Street when my crush, a college classmate, sent me a Dear John letter. She explained why she couldn't be with me, even though I was the man every woman would want. It's interesting how often relationships end with "It's not you, it's me." I couldn't even call it a relationship because we went on two dates. But at that moment, it was a big enough trigger to launch me into a spiral of emotions I didn't need. One of the evenings ended with me walking around with a bottle of whiskey in a pub a stone's throw from my home at the time. I do not remember trying to hurt people, but my memories are insufficient proof that this didn't happen. I must have stepped on somebody's toes because he pushed me hard and knocked the bottle out of my hand so it broke all over the pub garden.

I immediately headed home but realized I had been shot before reaching my flat's front door. Don't panic. I hadn't really been shot, just in my sick mind. To clarify what happened, I took a picture of the wound on my shoulder and posted it on Facebook. Then I found a colleague on chat and told him I was dying because someone had shot me. He responded in an exemplary manner and called 112—the emergency number. Fifteen minutes later, there were several police cars outside my window. I went down, told my story, and suggested that the shooter might be in my flat. For the first time in my life, I saw police officers with guns in hand, moving slowly toward the crime scene.

Of course there was no one in the apartment, but they still maintained their professionalism and took me to the emergency room, where I was to be examined by the doctor on duty. We got there, and I remember feeling important. Not everyone comes to the hospital with a police escort. The examination ended before it began. They put me in a cubicle where I was supposed to wait for the doctor, but I stumbled out. That's when my whole story came crashing down like a house of cards. The next stop was set. Ten minutes later, we parked in front of a psychiatric hospital. I remember being taken away in a police car, but it must have been an ambulance, like every time before. Anyway, the police officers went with me to the closed ward. That had never happened before, at least not that I knew of. Again, there was the bed strapping, the sedative to help me sleep, and the start of a new episode of my soap opera. It was nice while it lasted. The high was over. I braced myself for another plunge into the abyss of nothingness.

June 17, 2015—blog post

A few days ago, a man hit me. It popped, it glinted, and I flew away. When I saw the bloody hand, I was scared shitless. I'd never seen nor felt a bullet. I ran home, tended my wound, and showered. There was nothing. But I repeat, I've never felt a bullet. I had a bloody head and a wound on my arm. They took care of it. The police did everything they could. They escorted me to the entrance, guns in hand.

In shock, I went to the emergency room, where I was NOT treated. A policeman approached me and said, "Sign, and you'll stay a day." I didn't sign anything. I said, "I don't understand what I'm doing here." They tied me up. Me. Because I didn't do anything. Now I'm in a locked ward for a week, and I'm not happy about it. Shot or not, it's a disgrace.

Anyone who's a true friend will come to visit today. The rest of you no longer exist for me (figuratively). Visits are from 2 p.m. to 5 p.m.

Do your best! Please. I need hugs.

In practically every manic episode, I've encountered police officers in one way or another—whether I was directing traffic on the city's main roads or knocking on the door of an unsuspecting resident of a block of flats in the center of Ljubljana and asking him for a light and a glass of water. I don't find weirdos weird anymore because I know I was strange myself. But the police have always acted correctly when I was relatively normal or on the verge of blowing up. Every time. Some wanted to know what they could do if they encountered another manic person. I think I even gave one of the policewomen my book and told her to read it, and then give it to her colleagues at the station. I never found out whether she did, but it felt good. I conclude that the reasons for my good relations with the men and women in blue are that I've never made trouble around them, that I respect them, and that I know how to calm down quickly. As a result, I started going to the police station when things got out of hand with one of my manic swings. Or I ended up there by a bizarre combination of circumstances. In short, the police were my allies, and that feeling has remained to this day, even though I've not seen the inside of a police station for more than seven years.

One of my thoughts, when I think about past events and, consequently, dig inside myself and go back to repressed feelings, is that it could've been much worse. In a few situations, I've probably been quite lucky that it has ended the way it has. Luck and the ability to communicate that mania gave me. It's hard to believe, but I only got it in the snout once. That time when I wanted to run over a guy in old Ljubljana. Well, on another occasion I got punched in the stomach, and even then, it could have ended much worse, but I backed off in time. The other episodes, at least I think, passed without injury. I don't remember many things or I remember wrongly, and some stuff they probably didn't tell me. And it's better that way.

Anyway, on my tenth admission to the hospital, I was mentally prepared for another extended stay. But as fate would have it, my last holiday in Polje was the best one yet. I had so many visitors that they had to limit them. People I knew only through social networks came, and I had a free exit from the closed ward. It's common practice that you can go out at a specific time and for a limited period. I could go out whenever I wanted. I felt like a VIP.

But they knew (or were testing) how such a treatment would affect me. It turned out that the increased freedom did not carry me away; quite the opposite. And something else was different. They didn't knock me down, as I like to say. I landed very gently and continued from a much higher level than usual. I'm sure this was decisive not only for my treatment at the time but also for the further course of the disease.

JAKA TOMC

Tenth Time Is a Charm

:):

July 29, 2015

A thirty-four-year-old gentleman was admitted to our hospital for the tenth time because of an elevated mood, and his underlying illness worsened.

On admission, the patient was borderline agitated and loud, with an accelerated speech pattern and elevated mood. On admission, he was also uttering grandiose idealizations. He was completely uncritical of his condition. According to hetero-anamnestic data, he was hetero-aggressive in the domestic environment.

At the start of hospitalization, due to his inability to control his behavior in the face of the significant symptomatology of the disease with auto- and hetero-aggressive threats, a particular protective measure had to be introduced in addition to medical therapy. During his further hospitalization with us, the patient calmed down and became more cooperative and manageable. After adjusting the psychotropic treatment and administering depot therapy with olanzapine, the mood status gradually approached euthymia. The patient participated adequately in all ward activities, and we did not observe any peculiarities in the therapeutic outings to the domestic environment. As of today, he has been discharged to household care. At discharge, he is clear-headed, well-oriented in all respects, and of a well-ordered formal mind. His mood is euthymic. His affect is varied and genuine. The patient is free of psycho-productive symptomatology at discharge. He denies auto- and hetero-aggressive tendencies and is not at risk of suicide. He has established an appropriate critical attitude toward his condition.

Therapy at discharge: Abilify 30 mg, Quilonorm 2 x 450 mg, Depakine Chrono (500-0-1,000 mg), Zypadhera 405 mg i.m. every four weeks

* * *

Late in the summer of 2015, I was free again. I don't remember the weeks and months following my release very well. Reading emails, text messages, and social media posts and conversations is beneficial at times like this. But it's also true that reading archived messages, more often than not, makes me feel uncomfortable because I often realize how delusional I was at certain times. It's then that I come to terms with my bumpy memory and convince myself that some things are better left repressed, at least until I open them again by writing a book.

So I don't remember the summer, but soon autumn came, and with it, Her. My writing brought our lives together. We sniffed each other for a while, and then I plucked up the courage to invite her to my place. She came without any reluctance. She appeared at the front door with a bottle of rosé and a broad smile. We debated this and that about life and the universe, books and films, and the moon behaving suspiciously. When she left, we hugged, and that was that for that evening. There followed a few more visits to my place or hers, a visit to the Slovene football match between Olimpija and Maribor (football seriously marked our first years together), a trip to the ski-jumping tour in Bischofshofen, and on and on and on. Life had meaning again, and much-needed stability, and my mania faded with every passing day.

JAKA TOMC

How Do I Do It?

:):

Of course, I boast that I've been stable for many years. Why shouldn't I be proud of that? Alcoholics count the days, weeks, months, and (for the most persistent) years. Bipolar disorder is not similar to alcoholism? More than you think. I was a severe manic addict. My "abstinence" resulted from deciding at some point that mania wasn't good for me. Although many lovely things happen during manic phases, they always end similarly.

Is it really that simple? To decide, like you would give up cigarettes? No, it isn't. Again, several factors must come together for you to have the situation under control. When I publicly announced that I would keep my disorder at bay for five years, it lasted less than two weeks. But I stubbornly persevered, going to therapy and taking the medication they prescribed. That would probably not have been enough if I hadn't gotten my life in order. I no longer fought (so much) with my parents; I dismissed some friends from my life and welcomed Neja into it, who brought peace and stability.

Living with bipolar disorder is a constant struggle. There are periods of truce when I don't think about the illness and I live on autopilot, but it waits in ambush so I don't accidentally forget who I'm dealing with. I constantly fear being carried away, one way or the other. Sometimes I feel like a tightrope walker. A small mistake or an unexpected gust of wind and I'll hit the ground hard.

But it's not all bad. I've learned a lot from both the manias and the depressions. About the world, about the people who surrounded me then, and above all, about myself. I learned more about myself than I could've done if I hadn't had bipolar disorder. I learned about parts of myself that would probably otherwise have remained hidden. I looked into the abyss. I touched the clouds. I flew and fell and felt like an explorer stepping into uncharted territory. Like a space traveler who had set foot on a new planet. Like Jaka, who had discovered himself.

When I reminiscence about the periods of idleness that were sometimes the cause of an episode, sometimes the consequence, I realize that it's also work that keeps me somewhere in between. I have repeatedly told my psychiatrist that I have too much work to think about nonsense. What I meant by that was not that bipolar disorder is nonsense, but that I don't have time to think about all the things that could go wrong. When I was in an ashram in India, the foremost mantra there was physical work. They called it karma yoga. We did it daily, and it worked because I felt excellent.

Bipolar disorder is a lottery. Sometimes you hit a good day, and sometimes you hit a period when you're wading through the muck, but most of the time, you're walking a straight line that you think will never end. But it does. Every beginning has an end. One day there will be no more me, no more you, no more books, no more earth, no more universe. Everything will turn into nothing again for one reason—so it can begin again. This is called the circle of life. New bipolars will come after me with their problems and their victories. With their stories and their ideas. One of them may write a book. Perhaps they'll read mine and gather courage. Life is unpredictable. Let's be surprised and enjoy it as much as possible.

JAKA TOMC

Instead of a Happy Ending

:):

Once, after reading *Manic Poet*, my sister-in-arms told me that the book was good, but it was missing something. In her opinion, the ending should be happy; it should point the way out, or at least it should radiate optimism. Given that bipolar disorder is a chronic illness, often lifelong, it would be challenging to end the book with a miracle cure or a prescription for it. Today I feel well, I'm stable, and I'm free of the severe side effects of medication. Yet the threat of the disease breaking out again hangs over me like the sword of Damocles.

I'm doing everything I can to prevent this, but I'll probably never again be able to say I'm healthy. I'm not ill, but it isn't optimal. I've come to terms with the fact that I cannot feel great without risking an episode of mania and must not let myself go too low for too long because depression is constantly on the horizon. If I once wished for the good old Jaka of 2005 to return, today I know that the Jaka of 2023 is precisely what it should be.

My illness has shaped me into the person I am today, and I wouldn't trade my life and the experiences I've had along the way for anyone else's.

Although I do not feel happiness as before, I can safely say I'm content. I'm still dealing with the past and the future, but I'm learning to enjoy the present moment. Because if you think about it, that's all there is. There may indeed be a zero between plus and minus, but if you look at it carefully, it represents infinity. Let's enjoy discovering its vastness. Okay?

Hooray!

:):

You've reached the end of the book. Hooray!

If you liked it, would you be so kind as to rate and review it? It would mean the world to me.

Thank you!

If you have any questions or comments regarding the book or bipolar disorder, write to me at jaka@jakatomc.com.

JAKA TOMC

About Jaka

:):

© Mankica Kranjec

Jaka Tomc (1980) started writing when he was four. Soon he wanted to write his first story but was too occupied with kid stuff. Many years have passed, and he published his first novella in 2010. *Stop This Game* is his ninth published book and the third one to be translated into English.

He was manic when he gave his first interview and optimistically declared he would sell more books in Slovenia than Dan Brown. The challenge remains.

Jaka says he became a writer to avoid awkward conversations. He doesn't like small talk or phone calls. He loves genuine people who are not afraid to speak their minds.

Currently, he lives with his family in Ljubljana, Slovenia.

STOP THIS GAME

JAKA TOMC

Printed in Great Britain
by Amazon